Shakespeare & Social Engagement

Shakespeare &
Series Editor:
Graham Holderness, *University of Hertfordshire*

Volume 10
Shakespeare & Social Engagement
Edited by Rowan Mackenzie and Robert Shaughnessy

Volume 9
Shakespeare & the First Hamlet
Edited by Terri Bourus

Volume 8
Shakespeare & Biography
Edited by Katherine Scheil and Graham Holderness

Volume 7
Shakespeare & Money
Edited by Graham Holderness

Volume 6
Shakespeare & His Biographical Afterlives
Edited by Paul Franssen and Paul Edmondson

Volume 5
Shakespeare & the Ethics of War
Edited by Patrick Gray

Volume 4
Shakespeare & Creative Criticism
Edited by Rob Conkie and Scott Maisano

Volume 3
Shakespeare & the Arab World
Edited by Katherine Hennessey and Margaret Litvin

Volume 2
Shakespeare & Commemoration
Edited by Clara Calvo and Ton Hoenselaars

Volume 1
Shakespeare & Stratford
Edited by Katherine Scheil

Shakespeare &
Social Engagement

Edited by
Rowan Mackenzie and Robert Shaughnessy

berghahn
NEW YORK · OXFORD
www.berghahnbooks.com

First published in 2023 by
Berghahn Books
www.berghahnbooks.com

© 2023 Berghahn Books

Originally published as a special issue of *Critical Survey*:
volume 31, number 4, unless otherwise noted.

All rights reserved. Except for the quotation of short passages
for the purposes of criticism and review, no part of this book
may be reproduced in any form or by any means, electronic or
mechanical, including photocopying, recording, or any information
storage and retrieval system now known or to be invented,
without written permission of the publisher.

Library of Congress Cataloging-in-Publication Data

Names: Mackenzie, Rowan, editor. | Shaughnessy, Robert, 1962– editor.
Title: Shakespeare & social engagement / edited by Robert Shaughnessy
  and Rowan Mackenzie.
Other titles: Shakespeare and social engagement
Description: New York : Berghahn, 2023. | Series: Shakespeare & ; volume
  10 | Includes bibliographical references and index.
Identifiers: LCCN 2023020406 (print) | LCCN 2023020407 (ebook) | ISBN
  9781805390619 (hardback) | ISBN 9781805390633 (ebook)
Subjects: LCSH: Shakespeare, William, 1564–1616—Dramatic production.
  | Shakespeare, William, 1564–1616—Stage history. | Theater and
  society.
Classification: LCC PR3091 .S324 2023 (print) | LCC PR3091 (ebook) |
  DDC 792.9/5—dc23/eng/20230523
LC record available at https://lccn.loc.gov/2023020406
LC ebook record available at https://lccn.loc.gov/2023020407

British Library Cataloguing in Publication Data

A catalogue record for this book is available from the British Library

ISBN 978-1-80539-061-9 hardback
ISBN 978-1-80539-062-6 paperback
ISBN 978-1-80539-063-3 ebook

Contents

List of Figures	vii
Introduction Robert Shaughnessy	1
Chapter 1 **Thither and Back Again** *An Exploration of* A Midsummer Night's Dream Sue Emmy Jennings	7
Chapter 2 **Shakespeare in Yosemite** *Applied Shakespeare in a National Park* Katherine Steele Brokaw and Paul Prescott	17
Chapter 3 **Shakespeare's Fools** *A Piece in a Peacebuilding Mosaic* Maja Milatović-Ovadia	34
Chapter 4 **Getting it on its Feet** *Exploring The Politics and Processes of Shakespeare Outside the Traditional Classroom* Karl Falconer	51
Chapter 5 **'Branches of Learning'** *Collaborative Cognitive and Affective Learning Between Shakespearean Students trained in Schools, Universities and Carceral Institutions* Sheila T. Cavanagh and Steve Rowland	69

Chapter 6
    Producing Space for Shakespeare   85
    Rowan Mackenzie

Chapter 7
    Mind the Gap   107
    Working Across Lines of Difference in Carceral Shakespeare
    Frannie Shepherd-Bates and Kate Powers

Chapter 8
    Signing Shakespeare   130
    Tracy Irish and Abigail Rokison-Woodall

Chapter 9
    A World Elsewhere   147
    Documentary Representations of Social Shakespeare
    Susanne Greenhalgh

Afterword   161
    Rowan Mackenzie

Index   167

List of Figures

Figure 2.1. Shakespeare in Yosemite performs in the Half Dome Village (Curry Village) Amphitheatre, Yosemite National Park, 23 April 2017. Photo Credit: Shawn Overton.   18

Figure 2.2. Lee Stetson as John Muir performing in Shakespeare in Yosemite. Photo Credit: Shawn Overton.   25

Figure 2.3. Ranger Shelton Johnson plays the eagle bone flute during Shakespeare in Yosemite. Photo Credit: Shawn Overton.   27

Introduction

Robert Shaughnessy

The chapters in this volume began their life at the Applying Shakespeare symposium, co-hosted by the Shakespeare Institute (University of Birmingham), University of Kent and Guildford School of Acting, University of Surrey, which was held in Stratford-upon-Avon in March 2018. The first event of its kind in the United Kingdom, the symposium drew together scholars, service professionals, practitioners and participants in Shakespeare and applied and socially engaged theatre (an umbrella term for a range of performance forms, often in non-theatrical spaces and with an agenda of personal or social change) to consider how, when these two fields converge, the results can often be transformative for those involved. The contributions and conversations addressed Shakespeare in relation to a range of topics, including learning difficulties, diversity, disability arts, mental health, performance in custodial settings, therapeutic interventions, accessibility, social inclusion, pedagogy, relaxed performance and activism; all were fuelled by what Helen Nicholson has called 'an aspiration to use drama to improve the lives of individuals and create better societies', and by the conviction that 'applied

Notes for this section begin on page 6.

drama is primarily concerned with developing new possibilities for everyday living rather than segregating theatre-going from other aspects of life'.[1] James Thompson raises the stakes even further: theatre, like all good art, is a matter of joy, and 'participation in the joyful', he urges, 'is part of a dream of a "beautiful" future, in the sense that it becomes an inspirational force', acting 'to make visible a better world'.[2]

Socially engaged Shakespeare, in this setting, takes its place alongside the diverse array of performance practices that grew out of the politically engaged, educational and community theatre activities of the final decades of the twentieth century; as the articles in this volume reflect and the symposium participants recognised, the encounter between a canonical cultural force that has been both revered and contested and work that frequently characterises itself as egalitarian, inclusive and anti-elitist is by no means a simple or straightforward one. If access to Shakespeare's work, especially for those groups or individuals habitually excluded from it, is readily acknowledged as something akin to a universal cultural (even human) right, it can also equally readily lend itself to narratives of Shakespeare's anodyne universality; sometimes it is worth asking how much the perceived transformative power of Shakespeare in performance lies in the former term (Shakespeare) rather than the latter (performance). At the same time, we should remember that all Shakespeare is, in its own way, socially engaged, to the extent that it will be concerned with the needs and interests of its audiences, whether this be the relatively narrow demographic served by the Royal Shakespeare Company in Stratford-upon-Avon, or the rather more diverse group of theatre-goers that attend the reconstructed Shakespeare's Globe on London's South Bank. One of the aims of this volume is to offer a space for the stories of audiences that have largely been excluded from existing accounts of Shakespeare's performance history.

The collection contributes to a growing body of performance scholarship addressing Shakespeare as a socially engaged phenomenon. While the literature on Shakespeare and pedagogy is extensive and long-established, other applications have more recently begun to attract sustained and widespread attention. Shakespeare in prisons, for example (especially in the United States), has been the subject of numerous writings, a biennial conference and a number of book-length studies;[3] Shakespeare's potential for those working with neurodiversity (including autism and dementia) has also attracted interest.[4]

Sue Emmy Jennings opens with an imaginative exploration of *A Midsummer Night's Dream* from the long-term perspective of a theatre practitioner and dramatherapist, paying particular attention to the play's scope for engagement with dream states and altered consciousness, and focusing on her work with the Senoi Temiar peoples in Malaysia. Drawing upon psychotherapeutic accounts of child attachment and development, Jennings finds strong resonances between these and the parent–child conflicts, and their resolution, in Shakespeare's play: *Dream*, she suggests, offers a structure of journey and return, from order to controlled chaos and back again, that mirrors the imaginative trajectories of dreamwork and trance. In Jennings' account of *Dream*, the forest is less a literal than a metaphorical space; for Katherine Steele Brokaw and Paul Prescott, the real-world sylvan environment of Yosemite National Park is the setting for the annual outdoor, site-specific productions of Shakespeare staged to mark both Shakespeare's birthday and World Earth Day. Focusing upon the inaugural 2017 production, an hour-long collage of Shakespearean texts and excerpts from the work of early eco-activist John Muir, Brokaw and Prescott offer this as an instance of how Shakespeare can be creatively mobilised in the service of environmental awareness and activism. Invoking the performance anthropologist Dwight Conquergood's modelling of the 'three C's' of applied and socially engaged theatre (Creativity/Imagination, Critique/Inquiry and Citizenship/Intervention), they argue that the 'instrumentalisation' of Shakespeare for social ends enhances rather than diminishes its aesthetic value and power.

In this respect, their position aligns with that of Thompson, cited above; it is worth noting that Thompson's own insistence on the primacy of the aesthetic in applied theatre (an emphasis he describes as a shift from *effect* to *affect*) was shaped not just by arguments within the field but, more importantly, by the traumatic personal experience of an applied theatre project that he ran at a rehabilitation centre for surrendered child soldiers in Sri Lanka in 2000, which several months later was the scene of a massacre.[5] The place of applied performance, and of Shakespeare, in a former war zone is also the focus of Maja Milatović-Ovadia's chapter, which documents her work with the charitable organisation Most Mira (Bridge of Peace) in Bosnia-Herzegovina, and in particular the project *Shakespeare's*

Fools, mounted in 2013 and 2014, which made use of Shakespeare's comedies to bring together ethnically-segregated school pupils as a contribution to the peace and reconciliation process. Shakespeare's work in this context, precisely because it did *not* directly confront the war and recent history, offered participants in the project a safe space which enabled them to begin to renegotiate the legacy of recent atrocities, and to glimpse future possibilities of peaceful co-existence.

Shakespeare for young people beyond the structures of formal education is the subject of Karl Falconer's chapter, the first of five chapters addressing the uses of Shakespeare in both formal and informal pedagogic settings. Reflecting on the work of his Liverpool-based PurpleCoat company, Falconer argues that a performance-based mode of Shakespearean pedagogy encourages access to the works for those individuals and communities who, by virtue of gender, race and, especially, class, are frequently alienated by, or excluded from them. As Falconer recognises, engaging working-class young people with Shakespeare is a complex business, fraught with ambivalence, on the one hand an opportunity for empowerment and enrichment, on the other a means to take ownership of cultural capital. Questions of access and ownership also inform Sheila T. Cavanagh and Steve Rowland's account of their involvement in an educational collaboration between undergraduate students at Emory University, Atlanta, and the inmates of Monroe Correctional Facility, Washington State, whereby the two groups study Shakespeare alongside and in dialogue with each other. Examining the points of convergence and difference between the expectations and experiences of incarcerated and non-incarcerated students, Cavanagh and Rowland show how, for the latter especially, the more extreme content of Shakespeare's plays (family dysfunction, violence, murder) is often painfully reminiscent of personal histories; reflecting preoccupations that have become newly urgent in the wake of the Black Lives Matter movement in the United States and elsewhere, they also highlight the importance of race to the carceral experience, and to these histories. The shared Shakespeare programme, they suggest, changes student perceptions of the incarcerated as well as prisoners' perceptions of students and themselves, and can play an important role in the rehabilitation process. Rowan Mackenzie's chapter, which follows, extends and develops the investigation of prison Shakespeare within the UK context, deploying Henri Lefebvre and Michel Foucault's theorizations of physical and institutional space to examine an ongoing initiative at HM Prison Leicester. Originating in a two-week arts festival, Talent Unlocked, in 2017, this project centred on *Othello*, initially on the grounds that its representation of sexual jealousy would resonate with inmates separated from their partners; as the work progressed, Mackenzie documents, members of the project found in Shakespeare both a means for self-exploration and a space for thinking beyond the confines of the prison regime. Writing from the perspective of prison-theatre facilitators and educators, Frannie Shepherd-Bates and Kate Powers address the implications of gender for the work that can be undertaken within carceral regimes in the United States, reflecting on the different kinds of activity and strategies of engagement that are possible or necessary when working with male and female inmates. They place a particular value on the capacity of Shakespeare work to accommodate not just a plurality of viewpoints but also the quality of ambiguity, something rarely entertained within the prison system.

Applied Shakespeare, as mentioned above, includes a strong element of engagement with users and communities whose diversity is marked by difference or disabilities of various kinds. Tracy Irish and Abigail Rokison-Woodall's chapter details one such initiative in an account of their work with Shakespeare for the d/Deaf community, the outcome of an ongoing collaboration between the Shakespeare Institute and the Royal Shakespeare Company. Much more than an access programme for deaf participants, 'Signing Shakespeare' is also a celebration of the potential of signing to enrich, diversify and transform the language(s) of Shakespeare itself – a potential inherent, in different ways, in all of the activities and interventions covered in this book.

In the final chapter, Susanne Greenhalgh offers a perspective that also applies, to varying degrees, to all of the contributions in this issue. Addressing the television documentary subgenre that concerns itself with applied Shakespeare stories, Greenhalgh anatomises its prevailing tendency towards narratives of self-realisation and self-discovery, rehabilitation and redemption. Examining a range of examples that include Hank Rogerson's well-known *Shakespeare Behind Bars* (2005) and William Jessop's BBC documentary *Growing Up Down's* (2015), which follows Blue Apple Theatre Company's production of *Hamlet*, Greenhalgh identifies the filmic mechanisms that produce and reinforce the message that Shakespeare can create quasi-therapeutic, highly individualized solutions to problems that might be better seen as intractably social and political. By highlighting applied Shakespeare as a subject of representation in itself, Greenhalgh concludes by returning us to the question implicitly posed by Nicholson and Thompson: how can Shakespeare contribute to new ways of thinking and doing not just theatre but everyday life? chapters in this volume offer a sample of the range and variety of work that seeks to answer it. As both the scholarly discipline and theatre practice continue to develop and promote a more diverse and inclusive approach to their own activities, this work can only grow in importance.

Robert Shaughnessy is Professor of Theatre and Director of Research at Guildford School of Acting, University of Surrey. He has published extensively on Shakespeare in performance on stage and screen, contemporary drama and British theatre history. His most recent books are *Shakespeare in Performance: As You Like It* (2016) and *Shakespeare in the Theatre: The National Theatre, 1963–1975* (2018).

Notes

1. Helen Nicholson, *Applied Drama: The Gift of Theatre* (Basingstoke: Palgrave Macmillan, 2005), 3–4.
2. James Thompson, *Performance Affects: Applied Theatre and the End of Effect* (Basingstoke: Palgrave Macmillan, 2009), 2.
3. See, for example, Jean Trounstine, *Shakespeare Behind Bars: One Teacher's Story of the Power of Drama in a Women's Prison* (Ann Arbor: University of Michigan Press, 2004); Amy Scott-Douglas, *Shakespeare Inside: The Bard Behind Bars* (London: Continuum, 2007); Niels Herold, *Prison Shakespeare and the Purpose of Performance: Repentance Rituals and the Early Modern* (Basingstoke: Palgrave Macmillan, 2014); Rob Pensalfini, *Prison Shakespeare: For These Deep Shames and Great Indignities* (Basingstoke: Palgrave Macmillan, 2015); Rowan Mackenzie, *Creating Space for Shakespeare: Working with Marginalized Communities* (London: Arden Shakespeare, 2023). The Shakespeare in Prisons Conference was launched at the University of Notre Dame in 2013.
4. See Robert Shaughnessy, '"All Eyes": Experience, Spectacle and the Inclusive Audience in Flute Theatre's *Tempest*', in *Shakespeare: Actors and Audiences*, ed. Fiona Banks (London: Arden Shakespeare, 2018), 119–138; 'The Wind and the Rain: Facing Dementia in *Lear/Cordelia* and *The Garden*', in *Performing Psychologies: Imagination, Creativity and Dramas of the Mind*, ed. Nicola Shaughnessy and Philip Barnard (London: Methuen, 2019), 85–98.
5. Thompson, *Performance Affects*, 15–42.

Chapter 1

Thither and Back Again

An Exploration of *A Midsummer Night's Dream*

Sue Emmy Jennings

Interactive play and child development

Neuro-Dramatic Play (NDP) is the developmental paradigm that I have created for therapy, education and parenting, which includes sensory play, messy play, rhythmic play and dramatic play.[1] There is a sense of performance and heightened dramatic expression between mothers and babies. It is influenced by my research with a Malaysian tribe, the Senoi Temiar. Through sensory play, all our senses are developed: we don't just see the world and others, we hear, taste, smell and sense in the totality our experiences. We are alert both to dangers and to opportunities, to destructiveness as well as creativity. Messy play is essential if we are to develop form, and it is not helpful for young children to have adult ideas of form imposed on them. A three-year-old grandson coloured an outline of a snowman in purple, for the Christmas card for his mum. The kindergarten teacher said it was incorrect, and I'm pleased to say that his mother rang the

Notes for this section begin on page 16.

teacher and said he could colour snowmen any colour he wished. Rhythmic play continues the rhythmic experience of the baby before he or she was born, when babies are aware of their mother's heartbeat and the rhythms of her day-to-day life: walking, sleeping, dancing, rocking and so on.

As Kelly Hunter points out, the iambic pentameter of Shakespeare's verse can soothe and calm children (and teachers) who are aroused or nervous. In her work with children and young people on the autistic spectrum, she has created the Heartbeat Circle in which children and adults sit in a circle and with a closed hand beat on their heart while saying 'Hel-lo', both as a group and individually. Once the beat is established, the game develops facial expressions, emphasising how a feeling *looks*. She suggests that:

> Shakespeare's language, his definition of love, explores how it *feels* to be alive whilst he uses the rhythm of the heartbeat to reveal the ever-changing specificity of those feelings; the rhythm is the *life* of the feeling.[2]

Although she is specifically referring to work with children on the autistic spectrum, when she describes how they need help with expressing feelings, making eye contact, accessing their mind's eye and their dreams, her methods are equally relevant to children with developmental delay, behavioural challenges and emotional struggles.

Playing with Shakespeare's verse, rhythm and stories is relevant for all children, as I witnessed when I developed a project of *Dream* in a village primary school in Somerset a few years ago. The project integrated children aged four to eleven, and even found a place for one young child who was a screamer. I asked him to scream when we needed it and signalled him when the workmen disappear as they see Bottom with the ass's head. He experienced an appropriate moment for his screams, contained within the parameters of the scene:

> O monstrous! O strange! We are haunted! Pray masters!
> Fly, masters! – Help
>
> (3.1.98–99)

And a few lines further on:

> Bless thee, Bottom! Bless thee! Thou are translated.
>
> (3.1.112)

Dramatic interactive play develops from birth, with expressions between mother and baby, echoing sounds and imitation of feeling faces. New-born babies imitate the expression on their mother's face within a few hours of birth; they are 'dramatising' before they begin language. If we observe mothers and small babies playing, they often seem to be in another world. 'Other worlds' is a theme that permeates Shakespeare's plays and one which I believe is important for mental health. We need to experience our imagination, and interactive/dramatic alternative states of being, in order to achieve balance.

Usually, these stages of NDP (sensory/messy play, rhythmic play and interactive dramatic play) are complete by six months old, and then wider spheres of playing unfold: movement and rhythm, making and creating (pictures and models), story and drama. These build a solid basis of play for the first six years, when children then make the transition from dramatic playing to 'drama for real'. Children develop a sense of performance and appropriate characterisation. The children who have navigated their early play development will now have a sense of dramatic timing as well as beginning to appreciate the rhythm, metre and metaphor in Shakespeare's texts.

> Why you must not speak that yet; that you answer to Pyramus.
> You speak all your part at once, cues and all.
>
> (3.1.91–93)

It is now that the child begins to understand the balance between reality and imagination, the 'let's pretend' and 'this is how it is'. In Romania, I was working with a large group of young men and teenagers who were rough sleepers.[3] Having been told a local folk tale that could have several endings, the instruction was to create their own ending. One young man became very agitated and pulled my sleeve, saying, 'The wolf doesn't really eat Mihai the shepherd boy, does he? He doesn't really eat him?' He was unable to keep the fiction, what I call 'dramatic reality', and it spilt into everyday life. I will return to this topic below.

Shakespeare was well used to the idea of 'the play within the play' and the metaphor of the actor, performer, stage and theatre as a mirror of humanity. In *Dream* he goes further with his life metaphors in relation to the phases of the moon and the confusion between reality and imagination, the here and now, and the dream time:

> Are you sure
> That we are awake? It seems to me
> That yet we sleep. We dream
>
> (4.1.192–193)

I feel passionate about early child development through playful and imaginative attachment, and also Shakespeare's plays. Since the former is the basis of a child developing security and imagination, it becomes the forerunner of participation in the poetry, stories and drama of Shakespeare.

Shakespeare makes his own pithy comment on the stages of life, but makes a leap from the infant 'mewling and puking' to 'schoolboy unwillingly to school'. However, he makes use of the word play in a myriad of ways, from player and playhouse, to play and sexuality, play as disguise, play and madness, play and the Fool. The most playful character in *Dream* is the anarchic Puck, who plays, jokes, teases, disguises, changes into animals and people. Puck is almost like a stage manager who organises everyone in their scenes and characters. He has a kind streak towards the lovers when he makes sure they are all reconciled at the end. But he also says to Oberon, 'Lord what fools these mortals be'. He and Oberon are entertained by all the muddles of the lovers, until Oberon gets angry that he has gone too far: 'This is thy negligence' (3.2.345). The playing has been overdone: 'tears before bedtime'.

Emotional intelligence: attachment, empathy and resilience

The argument between adult and youngster, when Puck explains how he got it wrong and Oberon decides to take action to reverse the mistakes, is a good example of 'role-modelling'. Both of them communicate very clearly and listen to each other. This is just one simple example of Shakespeare providing learning for emotional intelligence. In many scenes, the interaction between younger and older characters provides examples of appropriate and inappropriate communication.

Attachment is crucial for healthy child development, and *Dream* illustrates many forms of attachment. Attachment is explored between parents and children, parents and teenagers, lovers and would-be lovers. Oberon and Titania have very strong attachments to their bands of youthful followers. Despite their occasional bickering, the workmen have a strong group attachment. Once their arguments are resolved, Titania and Oberon rediscover their attachment. We never learn, though, how Egeus feels when his only daughter becomes attached to a man of her own choosing. Empathy is demonstrated in some characters and its lack in others. Theseus is much more empathic than Egeus, for example. He allows time to elapse to help Hermia herself resolve the conflict as to whom she will marry. Her father wants her put to death right away if she does not obey his choice. Egeus is a complex character and appears to be rigid and bitter. Titania and Hippolyta both show a lot of empathy towards the dilemmas of the lovers and the plight of the orphaned Indian boy.

Resilience is a means of dealing with the ups and down of life without being overwhelmed when challenged. Egeus again (he is an underexplored character) shows excessive rage when his daughter does not obey him. His threats get more and more extreme, and it is Theseus who is conciliatory. Among the workmen, Peter Quince asserts calm control while others are shooting off at tangents, especially Bottom. But even Quince has concerns that the ladies might shriek at the lion – and that could be enough to hang them all. Nevertheless, the group show enough resilience to overcome all difficulties, including Bottom's temporary 'translation', sufficiently to perform their play.

The Temiar are very clear about the need for calm, and children are discouraged from playing in a boisterous way. They believe that it is not a good idea to attract the attention of negative other-world beings, in particular their arch-enemies of 'tiger' and 'thunder', which have the power to destroy and annihilate. However, the strongest shaman is the one who can 'meet' the tiger without being destroyed. In the tiger healing séances, they believe the shaman turns into a tiger. The 'tiger' is contained within a small shelter, built for the purpose within the main house. The energy of the tiger is considered too powerful to be contained within the ordinary house. The performance is managed by an assistant, rather like Puck, who makes sure everything is in its place, that the lights are down, the fire and music muted.

Ritual and theatre

The balance between ritual and theatre ensures that we feel secure on the one hand through the shared symbols of cultural rituals, while we can also be challenged and enervated through witnessing theatre. The power of theatre is at its strongest when it is Shakespeare. No other writer for theatre has been able to create the depth of experience, the powerful metaphor and the strong resolutions. Small infants need the secure attachment of life being predictable, and paradoxically will then feel confident to take risks. For children who experience life as chaotic with no secure respite, they are likely to feel anxious or nervous and in need of calm. I maintain that 'babies feel calm in arms'. *Dream* starts with the unyielding rules of the court, the journey into the chaos of the forest and the return to order but with some compromises.

Whether we are seeing the play at the theatre or participating in a project at school, the structure is the same – the journey from order to chaos and challenge, and back again. Most performances have a ritual structure as we 'settle' as audience, engage with what is going on in front of us, where we are challenged, surprised, angered and loved, before the gradual closure and return to everyday life. The conventions of theatre do not allow us to leave in a hurry, and we witness the performers becoming themselves again, and show our appreciation or otherwise, before walking away. With the Temiar people, the shaman is not only healer, but entertainer, philosopher, social leader and counsellor. After a healing séance, performers transform into themselves again, although very bleary and disorientated. Everyone stays until dawn and they emerge into daylight to return home.

In my rainforest research I witnessed several variations of their established shamanic traditions. The shamans are of various grades from minor to major, and very rarely the great shaman. The great shaman, it is believed, can actually metamorphose into a tiger, the most feared and dangerous creature. Such a shaman can embody the extreme of danger and during this entranced period become a very powerful healer. As described above, a special hut is constructed inside a domestic house in which the shaman will turn into a tiger. We are alerted to this when there is a scratching on the branches that form the shelter, believed to be the tiger's claws, accompanied by a soft growling. It is a very deep emotional experience that has a profound effect on the well-being of everyone present.

The tribe often refer to playful trance experience, using the expression 'to forget'; ordinary people as well as minor shamans 'forget', with the younger people dancing ecstatically and the older men gently rocking. People who are ill, or parents of new-borns, do not go into trance as it is believed it will endanger their head-soul. It is considered that when in trance, the head-soul leaves the body and goes on a journey, sometimes to play with other head-souls or to discover a new dance, song, hunting destination or cure. The trance state is one of creativity and discovery, which in turn is shared with the community. An ethos of sharing, whether from this world or the other, is the foundation of this tribe's social structure.

As the audience, we have been on a journey from everyday to dramatic reality, and back to the everyday. The skilled therapist or theatre director ensures that the return journey is secure, with some kind of resolution. We have lived the emotions in this journey, which have been communicated to us through the actors. As Puck says in his closing speech, we must remember that the actors are shadows and if we feel uncomfortable then we can decide that we have been dreaming. Puck gives us autonomy to take the story on board, or not.

Struggles and conflicts

In the community, education and therapy, we often need to face up to the struggles of life. In ancient times the theatre served that very purpose. Every culture has great theatre or dramatic rituals that provide the opportunity for witnessing or addressing challenges or conflicts, in symbolic form. Dramatic rituals are also about consciousness raising and about empowerment. People are empowered to challenge the wrath of the gods, seek healing for dangerous illness, become successful hunter-gatherers or entrepreneurs. Rituals give us strength to develop autonomy so that we can deal with the day-to-day travails of living.

Titania addresses this succinctly when she is challenging Oberon on their disagreement about the Indian boy; the scene illustrates well the type of domestic conflict when a child is in the middle of two warring parents. Titania points out that there is chaos for mortals when the fairy characters are at war; when there is dissent in the 'other world', humans are insecure and disorientated.

> These are the forgeries of jealousy:
> And never, since the middle summer's spring,
> Met we on hill, in dale, forest, or mead,
> By paved fountain, or by rushy brook,
> Or in the beached margent of the sea,
> To dance our ringlets to the whistling wind,
> But with thy brawls thou hast disturb'd our sport.
> Therefore the winds, piping to us in vain,
> As in revenge, have suck'd up from the sea
> Contagious fogs which, falling in the land,
> Hath every pelting river made so proud
> That they have overborne their continents.
> (2.1.81–92)

She goes on to describe how the crops have rotted, sheep are dying and the crows feed well on the corpses, and the humans need their winter cheer. There is dissent in fairy land, which creates destruction on earth. And it is not just dissent. She describes a lack of playfulness, dance and music that brings about 'contagious fogs' and floods. The earlier playfulness of Puck and one of the junior fairies contrasts with the conflict in the heavens, and shows the broad influence of 'other-world' characters and scenes on us as audience or participant.

The Temiar shaman makes sure that tension does not escalate in the village. If people get 'edgy', there is a séance. They believe in peaceful co-existence and no violence. If there are conflicts, people sit down and discuss them. For the Temiar, life must be fair.

Consciousness and altered states

Throughout *Dream* we are moved through different states of consciousness and theatre. The workmen are rehearsing a play, within the play, and they are disrupted by Puck putting the ass's head on Bottom. Meanwhile, Oberon has entranced Titania by putting love juice on her eyes so that she falls in love with the 'translated' Bottom. Her love language while entranced is extremely beautiful; the challenge to us as audience is that she is expressing it towards someone described as 'gross' and 'monstrous'. Titania and other characters have journeyed into trance and back again.

Puck and Oberon are very much aware that they are different from the mortals and conduct most of their activities in darkness, and it is Puck who reminds Oberon that they must finish all their plans 'with haste' (3.2.278). But as Oberon reminds him, 'But we are spirits of another sort' (3.2.288). Puck also differentiates between ghosts, those who have somehow wandered out of their graves and those who have killed themselves and have been buried at crossroads instead of in consecrated ground.

The play allows us to explore difference: court characters, work people and fairy folk; young people and old people; male and female; reality and fantasy; chaos and order; this world and other world; dreams and everyday; strangeness and truth; trance and reality – differences in time, space, consciousness, role and imagination. As Theseus says to his new wife Hippolyta:

> The lunatic, the lover, and the poet,
> Are of imagination all compact.
> (4.2.7–8)

It is this very nebulous state within 'dramatic reality' that allows people of all descriptions, whether the walking well or those with unwell being or social disadvantage or disability or those people restrained or contained in secure settings, to challenge their ideas of self and the world. The Temiars are a contemporary example of a culture that has built both prevention and cure in their forest through creative and artistic experience. This includes trance and performance. In Western Europe we need therapists and theatre to do this for us. Shakespeare's dangerous forest has other-world fairy characters that lead the mortals into unsafe places through transformational potions. The transition back to the safety of a now more human court with flexible borders, and market folk with their entertainment, completes the journey. Everyone is blessed by the other-world fairy folk and the audience is reassured that their shadow selves, portrayed by the actors, need not give offence. All will be well.

In his penultimate speech, Puck, who is a rule-maker as well as a rule-breaker, describes his role of ultimately tidying everything away. But in this speech he also reminds us of the darkness and the shadows. The house he is referring to is not the Duke's palace, but the theatre, which is often referred to as house (notices outside will say 'House full'). In this speech and the final one, Puck is reassuring the audience that it can be safe from disturbance (and mice). He also says that it is a hallowed space, like the shamanic sacred space:

> Now the hungry lion roars,
> And the wolf behowls the moon;
> Whilst the heavy ploughman snores,
> All with weary task fordone.
> Now the wasted brands do glow,
> Whilst the screech-owl, screeching loud,
> Puts the wretch that lies in woe
> In remembrance of a shroud.
> Now it is the time of night
> That the graves, all gaping wide,
> Every one lets forth his sprite,
> In the church-way paths to glide:
> And we fairies, that do run
> By the triple Hecate's team
> From the presence of the sun,
> Following darkness like a dream,
> Now are frolic; not a mouse
> Shall disturb this hallowed house;
> I am sent with broom before,
> To sweep the dust behind the door.
> (5.1.361–380)

All is well and all manner of things are well.

Professor Sue Emmy Jennings is Distinguished Scholar, University of the Witwatersrand, Honorary Research Fellow University of Roehampton. She has pioneered Dramatherapy and Neuro-Dramatic-Play in many countries including Malaysia and India. Her doctoral fieldwork 'Theatre, Ritual and Transformation' was conducted with the Senior Temiars. They inhabit the Malaysian rain forest, where she lived for eighteen months with her three children. She has published over fifty books and is currently researching 'Attachment in *A Midsummer Nights Dream*'.

Notes

To the Senoi Temiar for their welcome and honesty; to the dramatherapists who use Shakespeare.

Language: I am using the word tribe and tribal in the anthropological sense of a form of social organisation. It does not infer any discriminatory expression nor overtones of colonialism.

1. Sue Jennings, *Healthy Attachments and Neuro-Dramatic Play* (London: Jessica Kingsley, 2011).
2. Kelly Hunter, *Shakespeare's Heartbeat: Drama Games for Children with Autism* (London: Routledge, 2015). Emphasis in original.
3. Following the brutal communist regime of Ceauşescu (1948–1989), many children and young people ran away from the orphanages and slept in railway stations and under bridges. Nowadays there are still rough sleepers in Romania, as in the UK.

Chapter 2
Shakespeare in Yosemite
Applied Theatre in a National Park

Katherine Steele Brokaw and Paul Prescott

If twenty-first-century performance is marked by a re-engagement with meaning, politics and society through the creation of interactive encounters, as Andy Lavender has claimed, then no branch of Shakespearean theatre practice is more twenty-first-century, more of the present cultural moment, than Applied Shakespeare.[1] This article is about Shakespeare in Yosemite, a project co-founded by the authors that attempts to apply Shakespeare to the crises of environmental disaster and the exploitation of public and native lands.

In 2017, we produced the first Shakespeare in Yosemite on the weekend of Earth Day and Shakespeare's birthday. Earth Day is celebrated on 22 April each year and is, according to its organisers, 'the largest civic-focused day of action in the world'.[2] Our inaugural show was a one-hour performance splicing together scenes from Shakespeare with the prose of John Muir, the so-called father of the National Park System (Muir's birthday falls on 21 April, so the show

Notes for this section begin on page 31.

Figure 2.1. Shakespeare in Yosemite performs in the Half Dome Village (Curry Village) Amphitheatre, Yosemite National Park, 23 April 2017. Photo Credit: Shawn Overton.

was devised as a conveniently neat triple celebration of Muir, Shakespeare and the planet). In 2018, on the same late April weekend, we mounted a fully staged, eco-inflected production of *A Midsummer Night's Dream*, and returned in April 2019 to stage an environmentally sensitive version of *As You Like It*. The now annual project is co-sponsored and fully funded by our home institutions, UC Merced and the University of Warwick, as well as receiving in-kind support from the National Park Service. The shows feature and are co-created by students, local community actors, a few professionals and – crucially – have a range of inputs from park rangers and staff. In effect, then, Shakespeare in Yosemite offers public university-sponsored free outdoor Shakespeare to a general audience. It does so, furthermore, on a weekend when admission charges to this flagship national park are waived in honour of Earth Day. Shakespeare in Yosemite thus applies place-based Shakespearean theatre in the heart of Yosemite Valley to foreground themes relating to ecological crisis and to prompt individual and collective action in its audience.

In what follows, we will briefly outline our methods for creating and analysing this kind of applied theatre; describe how these performances are informed by eco-critical Shakespeare and eco-theatre practices; explain the particular context of Yosemite National Park and what we are trying to do there; and finally we describe and reflect on our inaugural 2017 show.

Methods and theories: applied theatre and eco-criticism

In conceptualising the various theories and practices involved in the project, we find the work of the late performance anthropologist Dwight Conquergood helpful. When articulating best practices for the field of performances studies, Conquergood identified three interwoven strands running through artistic, scholarly and community-engaged practices.[3] Conquergood's three 'C's – which are also partnered and glossed by three 'I's – are: (1) Creativity/Imagination; (2) Critique/Inquiry; and (3) Citizenship/Intervention.

The Creative or Imaginative element of our project includes the collaborative process of adapting Shakespeare's plays to new purposes, and working with a team of primarily student and community actors to rehearse and produce the shows. Crucial to these artistic endeavours is the priority to value the insights of collaborators who are not professional Shakespeareans: scientists, park rangers, activists, community actors.

Conquergood's second strand – Critique or Inquiry – involves research and analysis of the texts and contexts that ground our artistic work and activist intentions. This includes our engagement with the Shakespearean texts, performance and eco-critical scholarship, and the local contexts of the people and places involved. This strand also involves doing theatrical field work by taking note of how Shakespeare, our cast and production team, our audiences and the environments in which we perform are mutually impacted by our particular performance practices. In order to help us analyse this, we take rehearsal logs, interview and survey cast and crew members both in person and via email, and collect audience surveys.

Finally, the work aims to be what Conquergood describes as Interventionist, or engaging in Citizenship, which is to say that like all applied theatre, it hopes in some small way to make an impact on particular communities while addressing larger public concerns. As Helen Nicholson explains, one of the debates 'most regularly revisited with regards to community-based and applied theatre is that of artistry versus instrumentalism'.[4] James Thompson, for example, critiqued applied theatre in 2009, claiming that it pays insufficient attention to affective and aesthetic responses to performance.⁵ Nicholson and several other practitioners and scholars of applied theatre disagree with Thompson's assessment, and we do too. We find that instrumentalizing the theatre – in our case, Shakespeare – for particular public and social purposes can enhance rather than diminish affective and aesthetic effects. We also find it important to defend 'instrumentalisation' itself, for art projects with purpose – Shakespeare for ecology, for example – would be worth doing *even if* they were not as artistically accomplished as 'pure' projects without an applied aim. The notion that instrumentalising Shakespeare might cheapen or diminish his body of work is also misguided. To echo what we also claimed in an op-ed that ran in local newspapers the week of the 2018 performances,⁶ Shakespeare is the most robust and renewable cultural artefact around. We can plunder his texts without ever diminishing their aesthetic, affective and academic capacities, or spoiling them for future generations. By contrast, many of the Earth's material resources we are plundering are not coming back. If part of the failure of the modern environmentalism movement is narratological, the failure to tell the story of climate change, can Shakespeare lend a hand? We agree with Randall Martin and Evelyn O'Malley who suggest in their recent and timely special issue of *Shakespeare Bulletin* on Eco-Shakespeare in Performance that 'far from shying away from Shakespeare's canonicity, it seems worth trying to exploit it for whatever (limited) potential it may contain'.⁷ Indeed, we think that Shakespeare seems as capable as any drama of participating in what Theresa J. May calls 'ecodramaturgy', which is theatre-making that puts ecological reciprocity and community at the centre of its theatrical and thematic intent.⁸

To think of a project like Shakespeare in Yosemite as ecological is to think about not only the ecological content we both find in and project onto the plays, but also to consider the ecosystem of humans, animals, plants, water and rocks in which Shakespeare is currently produced. The word 'ecology' was coined by Darwinian biologist Ernst Haeckel to describe the study of an *oikos*, or dwelling place. Yosemite is home to a diverse system of flora and fauna, and to the Park staff who help maintain this ecosystem in hopeful cooperation with the millions of tourists, hikers and climbers who visit the Park each year. Ecological thinking de-centralises the human by recognising that people are part of wider networks of interdependence, networks including animals, plants and elements, and in our inaugural show we sought to use Shakespeare, as well as the writings of naturalist John Muir, to help us address the specific ecological contexts of our current political climate, of Earth Day, and of Yosemite National Park.

Thus, the theories and practices supporting Shakespeare in Yosemite correspond to Conquergood's categories in the following ways:

- Creativity: we write original work and heavily adapt Shakespeare (and other writers, when relevant); we assemble a team of theatre artists with whom we collaborate on creating a new piece of site-specific theatre.
- Critique: we research before writing or adapting; we take field notes and collect surveys during the process and after the performances.
- Citizenship: we address issues of global and local concern through free and accessible performances in a public space not usually associated with Shakespeare or theatre.

Shakespeare in the (National) Park

Eco-Shakespeare is perhaps at its most effective when it is a performance practice, albeit one that is indebted to academic theory and criticism. The field of eco-critical Shakespeare is growing, and contributes important theoretical and historicist work to the study of Shakespeare, which informs both our theatre practice and our teaching.[9] But we agree with Randall Martin when he argues that

> Shakespeare's greatest possibilities for becoming our eco-contemporary arguably lie not in academic discourse but in performance ... Because Shakespeare in modern performance continues to appeal to a wide range of hearts and minds, his plays wield affective and imaginative power for shifting personal convictions and behaviours in ways that pioneering ecologists such as Aldo Leopold recognised were essential for stirring up environmental complacency and motivating progressive action.[10]

Indeed, as Martin rightly emphasises, Shakespearean performance attracts a wide audience base, particularly in its many manifestations of free, outdoor performance, a tradition that is particularly strong in the United States following the pioneering work of Joe Papp in the late 1950s and the example set by his Public Theatre in offering free Shakespeare in the parks and boroughs of New York City. According to the Institute of Outdoor Theatre, the combined attendance at free outdoor Shakespeare in 2017 was 231,007, while 405,619 people paid some amount of money – often quite small – to attend outdoor Shakespeare.[11]

This tradition of outdoor performance means that Shakespearean events often call attention to how fields and trees and rivers and weather affect, indeed participate in, performance, and how the wider environment frames the lived experience of the human and non-human. Outdoor Shakespeare festivals can learn from the theories and practices of eco-theatre to create work in a productive relationship with the natural world. Indeed, performances of our 2018 *Dream* in Yosemite featured audience and actor interactions with a bobcat, blackbirds, a dog who barked back at Puck, and a passing family of mule deer who were echoed by the onstage fairy we had renamed 'MuleDeer', all of which encounters reinforced the ecological imperatives of the adaptation. As Martin points out, Shakespeare the playwright often draws audiences' attention to both the stage and the physical environment at large: environment isn't just decoration.[12] And that matters if you are looking out at a landscape like Yosemite Valley (see Figures 1–3).

But why put Shakespeare in this setting? We think that Shakespeare offers particular advantages to an art project focused on ecological advocacy. One of those relates to the work's hyper-canonicity. Despite periodic calls from practitioners for a moratorium on Shakespeare's plays, and despite the best historical efforts of anti-Bardolators like George Bernard Shaw, there is a commonly held perception in many cultures that the act of putting on a Shakespeare show requires little explanation or justification. This general consensus on the self-evident 'greatness' of the works partly explains their attractiveness to practitioners operating in repressive contexts. Unlike most new writing, Shakespearean performance is able to mask its other intentions and, as Lear might have said, its 'darker purpose' (1.1.34). It is thus able to get people who might not otherwise consider listening to messages about climate change and human consumption to contemplate, at least for a moment, these matters. When the current federal administration in the United States was full of climate change deniers who had even forbidden the National Park Service (NPS) to confront directly anthropogenic global warming in their policies and communications, Shakespeare allowed us to work with the park staff to address, obliquely but powerfully, issues that were being censored by the very federal organisations that should have been broadcasting their urgency.[13]

This 'Trojan Horse' Shakespeare was much discussed in the 2018 Applying Shakespeare symposium held at the University of Birmingham's Shakespeare Institute: over centuries, the works have acquired the capacity to bring together people from a variety of political perspectives who might not otherwise talk or collaborate, and can allow for an exploration of issues that participants and audiences might in other contexts resist. Shakespeare can attract more and different people into a space than projects that appear more experimental, edgy or postdramatic. Such projects sometimes run the risk of pre-filtering their audience by (in effect if not intention) appealing mainly to relatively narrow and socially homogenous groups.

In putting Shakespeare in Yosemite, we are bringing the Shakespeare in the park tradition to one of the most prominent spaces in the NPS. The mission of the NPS is to 'preserve unimpaired the natural and cultural resources and values of the National Park System for the enjoyment, education, and inspiration of this and future generations'.[14] The NPS is focused on preserving both cultural and natural resources, but Shakespeare in Yosemite hopes to remind people that these categories are not necessarily distinct, and in fact are often co-constitutive. Jessica Rivas is a UC Merced alumna and now a Yosemite Park Ranger, who played Snout the Wilderness Ranger in our 2018 production of *Dream*. In conversation with the cast at our first rehearsal, Rivas explained that the arts have played a long and crucial role in saving Yosemite and many of America's natural treasures from commercial exploitation. In the late nineteenth and early twentieth centuries, it was the descriptive writing of naturalists (especially John Muir), the dramatic canvases of landscape painters and the wide circulation of early photography that convinced lawmakers back East that Yosemite needed protection. Such representations were often guilty of effacing the Native American presence in these landscapes and presenting them instead as somehow pristine and untouched. We hope that Shakespeare in Yosemite joins in the tradition of using artistic and cultural production to protect the natural world, while also being sensitive to the South Sierra Miwok and Paiute peoples who have seasonally inhabited the area for millennia.[15]

In particular, we hope that the theatrical event deepens parkgoers' reflective experience in Yosemite. It is an explicit goal of the NPS to prompt visitors to reflect on particular environmental threats to the astonishing landscapes they see before them so that they may better understand wider threats to the planet as a whole. The Parks system is studded with information boards and texts that often end with an ethical imperative to the reader-visitor; for example, here is one from Sequoia National Park: 'Preservation of our wilderness and, in fact, all of our planet, is up to you and me'. Theatre can give active, dramatic form – words, sounds, *gestus*, moving bodies working in a particular environment – to these kinds of reflective experiences.

Thus, the material conditions of site-specific performance, the political conditions of the current federal administration, the recent environmental catastrophes that have affected Yosemite and California, and the long history of conservation, have all informed our first two ventures in Yosemite. We will now describe and quote our first production, the show that we have retrospectively titled *One Touch of Nature* (but which was simply called *Shakespeare in Yosemite* in 2017). The script and practices of this first production are one answer to the question Martin and O'Malley pose: 'How can Shakespeare ... become an ecological discourse on stage, as well as a model for environmental practices in the theater?'[16]

Shakespeare in Yosemite, 2017: *One Touch of Nature*

The project originated in two coincidences. The first occurred in spring 2016 when the authors, somewhat lost in Yosemite Valley, stumbled upon a small, evidently underused playing space. We would later learn this was the Lower River Amphitheatre and that it had, in effect, been closed since the severe flooding of Yosemite in 1997. Engirdled by beautiful pine trees, above which the granite walls of the valley soar skywards, this was clearly an ideal space for outdoor Shakespeare. But a quick online search revealed that there was little to no recent precedent for Shakespeare or any other kind of outdoor theatre-making in the Park.[17] Our biggest obstacle, therefore, was to get permission to produce a public performance in the Park, as rights for such projects are carefully protected in the understandable effort to limit commercial exploitation. This is where we were vastly helped by a second coincidence, this one relating to time rather than space. Noting that John Muir's birthday, World Earth Day and Shakespeare's birth/death-day follow one after the other, the idea of an eco-Shakespearean event began to take form. We then contacted Lee Stetson, Yosemite's most famous actor, who has been portraying John Muir in the Park and around the world for the past thirty-four years. John Muir was the Scottish-born naturalist, writer and activist whose writing about Yosemite and the Sierras and relentless haranguing of presidents and Congresses to protect them resulted in the formation of the National Parks system. Muir was a

Figure 2.2. Lee Stetson as John Muir performing in Shakespeare in Yosemite. Photo Credit: Shawn Overton.

huge fan of Shakespeare: he carried the works around with him on his epic journeys across California and Alaska, quoted from him extensively and force-fed the plays to his daughters. Paraphrasing *Troilus and Cressida*, Muir was fond of observing that, 'One touch of nature makes all the world kin'. At Muir's memorial service in 1914, Enos Mills – who had been inspired by Muir to found the Rocky Mountains National Park – said this: 'No one has ever written of Nature's realm with greater enthusiasm or charm. He has written the great drama of the outdoors. On Nature's scenic stage he gave the wildlife local habitation and characters; what he did with the wild, Shakespeare did with man'.[18]

As we immersed ourselves in Muir's prose works, it became clear that there were a number of productive thematic and stylistic parallels between his writing and Shakespeare's and that the Park coordinators might just be interested in a one-hour show on environmental themes as part of their Earth Day weekend offerings to the public. Armed with this idea and the encouragement of then UC Merced Chancellor Dorothy Leland and former NPS associate director Steve Shackleton, we gratefully received the blessing of Rangers Sabrina Diaz and Jamie Richards and the rest of the Park staff to perform in two venues: the Lower River Amphitheatre and in the larger playing space at Half Dome (formerly Curry) Village.

Collaging excerpts from Shakespeare and Muir, *One Touch of Nature* explored themes relating to climate change, the rights of animals and the commodification of the environment. The cast of eleven was onstage throughout, and were dressed casually in hiking trousers and 'Shakespeare in Yosemite' T-shirts, shifting between roles and narration as the script demanded. The only exception was Lee Stetson, who played Muir throughout in his trademark tweedy vest (and ample beard). Despite the size of audiences at Half Dome Village, actors' voices were not amplified and, partly because of this, the general style of acting was broad, presentational and interactive.

The show began with a prologue from a figure familiar to many Yosemite lovers. Ranger Shelton Johnson – author, interpretive park ranger and, along with Stetson, a star of the Ken Burns PBS documentary about the NPS – addressed the audience with a prose-poem he composed for the occasion:

> For Shakespeare, Yosemite was an unknown land that could only be visited in his dreams ... Yet he would've appreciated a landscape powerful enough to be its own theater, script its own drama without the agency of a dramatist; a play of granite, soil, plants, animals, and indigenous people with their own stories, legends, joy and heartache thousands of years before the outside world had ever heard the word Yosemite.

Shelton's prologue ended with the injunction, 'Let this cross-pollination [of Shakespeare, Muir, and the Valley] bear an exotic, but sweet fruit for all to taste!' and, over the next hour, we did our best via a sequence of scenes and speeches from Shakespeare, intercut with Lee's delivery of Muir's powerful prose. For example, Jaques' reported protestations about the slaughter of the deer of Arden – 'we / Are mere usurpers, tyrants, and what's worse, / To fright the animals and to kill them up / In their assigned and native dwelling place' (2.1.60–63) – was immediately echoed by Muir's words: 'How blind Lord Man is to the rights of all the rest of creation! It is a mean, blinding, loveless doctrine that teaches that animals were made only for man, to be petted, spoiled, enslaved, or slaughtered'.[19]

For the sake of balance, though, we also contrasted the two writers' representations of the shepherd's life, first hearing Corin on earning that he eats, and his great pride in seeing his ewes graze and lambs suck (3.2.64–67), then hearing Muir's strangely ill-tempered verdict: 'A sheep can scarcely be called an animal. An entire flock is required to make one foolish individual. Sheep brain must surely be poor stuff, eh? I cannot find the poetry of a shepherd's life: if flocks of sheep were hidden from me, I should rejoice'.[20]

Figure 2.3. Ranger Shelton Johnson plays the eagle bone flute during Shakespeare in Yosemite. Photo Credit: Shawn Overton.

There was lots of music – the cast gathered while singing 'Under the Greenwood Tree', sang and danced to 'The rain it raineth every day', and, in perhaps our only concession to Elizabethanism, a lutenist accompanied the songs and underscored throughout. And there was aural cross-pollination across time and space when Ranger Shelton Johnson joined in on an eagle bone flute, an instrument indigenous to many American peoples, including the Miwok who long called Yosemite Valley home.

After a playful sequence aimed at younger members of the audience, the show's final fifteen minutes zeroed in on more obviously political-environmental themes. It began with Muir on the capitalist exploitation of natural resources:

> Everybody needs beauty ... this natural beauty-hunger is displayed in everything from poor folks' window gardens to 'our magnificent National Parks' [quotes in original]. Nevertheless, like everything else worth while, however sacred and precious and well-guarded, they have always been subject to attack, mostly by despoiling gain-seekers – mischief-makers of every degree from Satan to supervisors, lumbermen, cattlemen, farmers, eagerly trying to make everything dollarable.[21]

There followed short extracts from *Romeo and Juliet* and *Timon of Athens* which echoed this disgust for making 'everything dollarable'.[22] And this rush to the economic bottom line, a narrator continued, can result in the loss of paradise. Suggesting that John of Gaunt's dying speech in *Richard II* sounds like something Muir could have said when lamenting the loss of Hetch Hetchy (a stunning valley in Yosemite flooded in 1923 to become a water reservoir for San Francisco), the narration switched back to Lee, who conflated Gaunt, Muir and his own present self, to deliver the lines:

> This earth of majesty, this seat of Mars,
> This other Eden, demi-paradise,
> This fortress built by Nature for herself...
> This blessed plot, this earth, this realm, this England – or this America –
> This land of such dear souls, this dear dear land...
> Is now leased out, I die pronouncing it...
> America hath made a shameful conquest of itself.
> (cf. 2.1.41–43, 50, 57, 68)

Spoken in the 'demi-paradise' of Yosemite Valley on the first Earth Day weekend under an administration more committed to gas and oil companies than the protection of federal lands, Shakespeare's (slightly adapted) words took on new meaning. Brokaw first got the idea to use this speech in the show when listening to a talk on the dangers of fracking by scientist and activist Sandra Steingraber, who itemised the ways in which hitherto public lands are being, in her words, 'leased out' to commercial interests. Important to the process of making Shakespeare in the world is the ways in which non-Shakespearean authorities such as Steingraber make us consider the relevance and resonance of Shakespeare's words in completely new ways.

More than six hundred people attended the show over four performances. A few came into the Park especially, on UC Merced–sponsored bus trips or because they'd read about it in newspapers and social media publicity, but most of the audience members just happened to be in the Park that weekend. They might have learned of the show via the free newsletter handed to every vehicle on entry to the Park or might simply have stumbled upon the performances while wandering around the Valley.

We hoped that the show's environmental messages resonated with our audiences, and encouraged them to fill out an online survey. Responses indicated that for a number of audience members this show had done some of the things we hoped it would. Several respondents talked about the way that Shakespeare's words, in particular, deepened their sense of place in the Park, making them more aware of their connection to it and need to protect it by giving them vocabulary and imagery to describe it. One wrote: 'I think it really made me realise how beautiful Yosemite is and how great it is to have words to describe it'. Another explained: 'We often forget the preciousness of [the Park's] beauties. We take it for granted, it has to be protected and cherished'.

Other audience members commented that the words of Muir and Shakespeare helped give them a long perspective on urgent modern environmental issues: '[I enjoyed] How the troupe wove Muir and Shakespeare together to create an historical perspective that is relevant on Earth Day 2017'. Or another wrote: 'I feel basic moral dilemmas that we face are exactly what Shakespeare's characters are faced with, plus he expresses these human struggles and aspirations with such a depth and delicacy'. Another added that the show made them think about how 'we certainly have a responsibility to this beautiful place'.

Some even explained the way that the play came back to them as they continued exploring the Park, fulfilling one of our hopes that the production would deepen the reflective experience of hiking through the landscape: 'We saw the play on our first day, but I had flashbacks to it as we spent time in the park'. Another spectator described the way that the play created a sense of an at least temporary community, enhancing the viewer's sense of ownership: '[It was] lovely to see a ranger and students and guests all involved with each other ... felt more accessible, like visitors are really part of the place'. The temporary community that formed for the performances contained both first-time visitors to the Park and what might be called connoisseurs of Yosemite. One of the former commented: 'My first time here and now I'm inspired to get more involved in the environment. One world and we need to look after it'. And a Yosemite regular wrote: 'We have been coming to Yosemite four times a year our whole lives, and we have never seen anything like this. We just spent four days hiking in the backcountry and feel so very lucky that we came back to the Valley in time to see this. We learned so much about Shakespeare and Muir!'[23]

While it is very difficult to track or measure the long-term impact of such experiences, these responses are nevertheless encouraging.

The particulars of Shakespearean (and Muirian) language and the accumulated gravitas that comes from a long historical perspective together make Shakespeare particularly helpful (at least for some audience members) in conveying ecological messages. And the fact that a theatrical encounter can activate a deeper sense of connection both to the Park itself and to the community of people who must advocate to protect that Park suggests that projects like Shakespeare in Yosemite can play their small part in inspiring the action that is necessary to save public lands and natural habitats.

Indeed, we hope that Shakespeare in Yosemite addresses Shannon Jackson's concern that applied art projects should 'imagine sustainable social institutions'. Jackson worries that much social and activist art is anti-institutional: 'when a political art discourse too often celebrates social disruption at the expense of social coordination, we lose a more complex sense of how art practices contribute to inter-dependent social imagining'.[24] It is important to us to highlight the public nature of Shakespeare in Yosemite and indeed our support for the (ever increasingly compromised) institutions that sponsor it: public universities and federally funded national parks on public lands.

Eco-critic Sharon O'Dair argues that 'ecocriticism of Shakespeare is presentist, but it must stretch beyond the presentist criticism of the past to find ways to be active in public policy, in changing the ways people live – now'.[25] We hope that in changing – even just minutely – the way that our casts and some audience members think about our responsibility to the environment, we are applying Shakespeare for some good. As one audience member put it: 'I didn't see any connections between Shakespeare and the natural world before this performance!' At one show, many of our audience members had come directly from a 'March for Science' – having marched for science, they sat down for some art – and, on World Earth Day, in a vexed and partisan political climate, the gap between the two cultures of arts and science seemed small indeed.

Katherine Steele Brokaw is Associate Professor of English at University of California, Merced. She is author of *Shakespeare and Community Performance* (Palgrave Macmillan, 2023), *Staging Harmony: Music and Religious Change in Medieval and Early Modern English Drama* (Cornell, 2016), co-editor of *Sacred and Secular Transactions in the Age of Shakespeare* (Northwestern, 2019) and editor of the Arden Performance Edition of *Macbeth* (Arden, 2019). She has acted, directed and adapted Shakespeare in a number of communities in the USA and Europe.

Paul Prescott has acted, adapted and taught Shakespeare in a range of countries and contexts. He is the author of *Reviewing Shakespeare: Journalism and Performance from the Eighteenth Century to the Present* (Cambridge, 2013), a critical biography of Sam Wanamaker for the *Great Shakespeareans* series (Bloomsbury, 2013) and, as co-editor and contributor, *A Year of Shakespeare: Reliving the World Shakespeare Festival* (Arden, 2013) and *Shakespeare on the Global Stage: Performance and Festivity in the Olympic Year* (Arden, 2015).

Notes

1. Andy Lavender, *Performance in the Twenty-First Century: Theatres of Engagement* (London: Routledge, 2016), 3 and *passim*.
2. See https://www.earthday.org/earthday/.
3. 'Performance Studies: Interventions and Radical Research', in *Cultural Struggles: Performance, Ethnography, Praxis*, ed. E. Patrick Johnson (Ann Arbor: University of Michigan Press, 2013), 41–42.
4. Helen Nicholson, *Applied Drama: The Gift of the Theatre* (Basingstoke: Palgrave Macmillan, 2005/2014), 5.
5. James Thompson, *Performance Affects: Applied Theatre and the End of Effect* (Basingstoke: Palgrave Macmillan, 2009), 6.
6. Katherine Steele Brokaw and Paul Prescott, 'Saving the Earth Needs All Hands on Deck, Including Shakespeare's', *Merced Sun-Star* and *Modesto Bee*, 11 April 2018, http://www.mercedsunstar.com/opinion/article208648669.html.
7. Randall Martin and Evelyn O'Malley, 'Eco-Shakespeare in Performance: Introduction', *Shakespeare Bulletin* 36, no. 3 (Fall 2018), 386.

8. May defines 'ecodramaturgy' in '*Tú eres mi otro yo* – Staying with the Trouble: Ecodramaturgy and the AnthropoScene', *The Journal of American Drama and Theatre* 29, no. 2 (2017), 1–18. See also Dierdre Heddon and Sally Mackey, 'Environmentalism, Performance, and Applications: Uncertainties and Emancipations', *Research in Drama Education: The Journal of Applied Theatre and Performance* 17, no. 2 (2012), 162–192; and Baz Kershaw, *Theatre Ecology* (Cambridge: Cambridge University Press, 2007). And for non-Shakespearean examples of ecodramaturgical applied theatre projects, see Syed Jamil Ahmed, 'Applied Theatre and Climate Change in Bangladesh: Indigenous Theatrics for Neoliberal Theatricks', in *Critical Perspectives on Applied Theatre*, ed. Jenny Hughes and Helen Nicholson (Cambridge: Cambridge University Press, 2016), 150–171; and Stephen Bottoms, 'The Agency of Environment: Artificial Hells and Multi-Story Water', in *Performance and Participation: Practices, Audiences, Politics*, ed. Anna Harpin and Helen Nicholson (London: Palgrave Macmillan, 2017), 167–188.
9. See, for example, Randall Martin, *Shakespeare and Ecology* (Oxford: Oxford University Press, 2015); Craig Dionne, *Posthuman Lear: Reading Shakespeare in the Anthropocene* (New York: Punctum Books, 2016); Lyn Bruckner and Dan Brayton, eds, *Ecocritical Shakespeare* (Aldershot: Ashgate, 2011); Gabriel Egan, *Shakespeare and Ecocritical Theory* (London: Arden Bloomsbury, 2015).
10. Martin, *Shakespeare and Ecology*, 167.
11. See https://outdoor-theatre.org/wp-content/uploads/IOT_Traditional_Summary_2017.pdf. It should be noted that these figures are conservative given that many theatre companies and festivals do not share attendance data with the Institute. One such non-reporting company is Chicago Shakespeare Theatre; their touring summer 2018 *Dream*, for example, was seen, for free, by over thirty thousand Chicagoans.
12. In Martin's words: 'Shakespeare's signature practice of drawing spectators' attention to the temporal and physical actualities of stage performance also encourages them to reimagine both natural and manmade environments not merely as the décor of his dramatic narratives, but as dynamic contexts that materially shape human and non-human relations and identities'. Martin, *Shakespeare and Ecology*, 8.
13. See, for example, Rob Hotakainen, 'NPS Chief Scraps Climate-Focused Order', E&E News, 31 August 2017, https://www.eenews.net/stories/1060059511.
14. This is the National Park Service's mission, which can be found on their website, https://www.nps.gov/aboutus/index.htm (last accessed 9 December 2019).
15. The long presence of indigenous people in Yosemite Valley was a theme of our 2018 *Dream*; we consulted with a few members of the South Sierra Miwok tribe on that production and hope to expand this collaboration in the future.
16. Martin and O'Malley, 'Eco-Shakespeare in Performance', 378.
17. Gordon Davis has told us about a memory of seeing *Twelfth Night* in Yosemite Valley around 1950; although we have not yet been able to do archival work on early twentieth-century performance in Yosemite, there has certainly been no Shakespeare in recent years. The nearest thing Yosemite has to an early modern, very vaguely Shakespearean event is the seven-course Bracebridge Christmas Dinner which, for three-and-a-half hours (and a charge of $380.44 per adult), 'transports guests to Old England'; see http://www.bracebridgedinners.com/.

18. William F. Bade, 'Reminiscence of John Muir by William F. Bade', *John Muir Reminiscences* 4, https://scholarlycommons.pacific.edu/cs-jmr/4. The end of this quote would make more sense if reversed (i.e. what Shakespeare did with man, Muir did with nature), but we preserve the words as Mills apparently spoke them.
19. *John Muir in His Own Words*, ed. Peter Browning (Lafayette, CA: Great West Books, 1988), 70.
20. This line from the play conflates two different pieces of Muir's writing which can be found in *John Muir in His Own Words*, 7, and *John of the Mountains: The Unpublished Journals of John Muir*, ed. Linnie Marsh Wolfe (Madison: University of Wisconsin Press, 1979), 29.
21. *John Muir in His Own Words*, 65.
22. These were Romeo's lines to the Apothecary (5.1.80–83) and an edited version of Timon's dissection of the transformative properties of gold (cf. 4.3.26–44), the speech that made such an impression on Karl Marx.
23. 'Shakespeare in Yosemite Response', Surveymonkey, 2017, surveymonkey.com/r/Z6FJCJC (accessed 8 May 2017). We have received an Institutional Review Board (IRB) waiver by UC Merced to conduct this research in the United States.
24. Shannon Jackson, *Social Works: Performing Art, Supporting Publics* (London: Routledge, 2011), 14.
25. Sharon O'Dair, 'Is It Shakespearean Ecocriticism If It Isn't Presentist?', in Bruckner and Brayton, *Ecocritical Shakespeare*, 85.

Chapter 3
Shakespeare's Fools
A Piece in a Peacebuilding Mosaic

Maja Milatović-Ovadia

> If we shadows have offended,
> Think but this, and all is mended,
> That you have but slumbered here
> While these visions did appear.
> (*A Midsummer Night's Dream*, 5.1.414–417)

Puck's lines are delivered by a chorus of twelve young people strung across the Omarska community theatre space. Lengthy applause. Forty young people storm the stage and bow. This was the end of a four-month-long theatre project entitled *Shakespeare's Comedies – A Midsummer Night's Dream* (2013), run by UK-Bosnian charity Most Mira, in collaboration with four ethnically segregated schools from the Prijedor area.

> Shakespeare in Omarska – how surreal that sounds... How many walls came down over the three months of Most Mira workshops while these beautiful kids were preparing the play – Hats off to every-

Notes for this section begin on page 48.

one – a group of great, brave, persistent people who are fighting to show our children that there is an alternative to the poison we are relentlessly feeding them.

Thus commented Refik Hodzic, director of communication at the International Centre for Transitional Justice in a Facebook post on 28 May 2013. Omarska is a small mining town in Northern Bosnia. During the war in Bosnia, the mine complex was transformed into one of the four infamous concentration camps in the Prijedor area.[1] It is from here that the images came of starving and tormented people that shocked Europe in 1992.[2] The Bosnian war was one in a series of conflicts that followed the break-up of Yugoslavia. It lasted from April 1992 to December 1995 and involved bestial atrocities, the deaths of over 100,000 people, the displacement of 2.2 million, genocide on a scale unseen in Europe since the Second World War, organised mass rape and systematic destruction of cultural heritage.[3] The war ended in November 1995 with the General Framework Agreement for Peace in Bosnia and Herzegovina, known as the 'Dayton Peace Accord', agreed in a US air-force base Right-Paterson. It was signed a few weeks later, on 14th December 1995 in Paris by all three parties involved in the conflict: Alija Izetbegović for the Republic of Bosnia and Herzegovina, Franjo Tudjman for the Republic of Croatia, and Slobodan Milošević for the Federal Republic of Yugoslavia; officially witnessed by the British Prime Minister John Major, German Chancellor Helmut Kohl, French President Jacques Chirac, Russian Prime Minister Viktor Chernomyrdin and the US President Bill Clinton. This was a document that stopped the bloody armed conflict but failed to bring peace to the country, it simply transferred it 'from the military to the political realm'.[4] The main preoccupation of the Dayton negotiators was to establish territorial, military and security agreements and to provide a constitution for a new state. It created a unique and very complex institutional governance system based on ethnonationalism,[5] 'making Bosnia the state with the highest number of presidents, prime ministers, and ministers per capita in the entire world'[6] and leading country in the political and economic deadlock.

A quarter of a century on, Bosnian society is still heavily bruised by the war. The progress of the reconciliation process is slow due to the ethnic division also embedded in the Bosnia-Herzegovina constitution provided by the Dayton Accord, one-sided official narration of the conflict, denial or relativisation of the war crimes, as well as factual manipulation in the school history textbooks used to drastically reshape history into the desired national paradigm.[7] Furthermore, everyday life is deeply affected by economic hardship, high levels of corruption and extreme youth emigration.[8] Reconciliation is a long and complicated part of the process of rebuilding a society after conflict. It begins 'when the parties in conflict start to change their beliefs, attitudes, goals, motivations, and emotions about the conflict, each other, and future relations.'[9] Reconciliation studies propose a variety of methods and strategies, focusing on three categories: political, economic and social.[10] They include apology, truth and reconciliation commissions, public trials, reparations payments, writing a common history, education, mass media, publicized meetings between representatives of the groups, the work of NGOs, joint projects and cultural exchanges. Further, the literature on reconciliation suggests that the process needs to challenge five aspects of social beliefs formed during the conflict: the justness of the group's goals that supported the conflict; de-legitimisation of the rival group; one-sided self-glorification of one's own group; the confrontational and hostile relationship with the past opponent; and understanding of conditions and instruments for achieving and maintaining peace. Reconciliation cannot be imposed, there are no ready-made manuals and every situation needs to be seen in its specific context.[11]

Most Mira (Bridge of Peace) is a small UK and Bosnia-based charity set up to support peacebuilding in the Prijedor municipality. Its work avoids direct political references and is centred upon arts projects with young people born after the war but growing up with its strong legacy of segregation. Young people belong to the second generation, they were not perpetrators, nor were they directly victimized by the war. However, they are growing up kept apart by ethnic barriers in a society deeply marked by war's heritage and segregation. Most Mira's work began in 2009 with the first of its annual youth arts festivals, designed to bring ethnically divided communities together by creating a safe space and avoiding an explicit political focus.[12] Four years later, when the organization had established itself within the communities and gained their trust, it developed ongoing yearly projects with a stronger focus on theatre and peacebuilding.[13] From the very beginning I have unexpectedly been part of the organization and over a period of ten years I have different roles as a theatre director, project manager, workshop facilitator and artistic advisor.[14]

In 2013, we initiated *Shakespeare Comedies*, a theatre project run in collaboration with four ethnically segregated schools from the Prijedor municipality. The schools that participated in the project were Vuk Karadžić, from the predominantly Serb-populated Omarska, Kozarac, from the predominantly Muslim-populated town Kozarac, Ćirilo I Metodije, from the predominantly Muslim-populated Trnopolje, which suffered ethnic cleansing in 1992, and Branko Radićević from the now predominantly Serbian town of Prijedor. The project's community aims were to facilitate the encounters between young people of different ethnic backgrounds, to involve them in a non-hierarchical collaborative creative process and to create an opportunity for them to cross the invisible borders and to physically experience each other's surroundings. The artistic aim was to use a fictional narrative, specifically a comedy, and to grasp the quality of theatre as a collective and complex art form.[15]

The value of theatre within the post-conflict context lies in its potential to challenge, construct and deconstruct different narratives while offering space for multiple positions without enforcing the pretention that conflict should be resolved. Most theatre practitioners that are working in post-conflict settings have a similar understanding of the theatre's diverse purpose. Theatre is often recognised as an ethical space for creating and reflecting on memories and narratives; redefining social rules and ethical relationships; relating the experience of the groups to their cultural, social and historical contexts, developing relationships and communications in divided societies, and figuring empathy and affect.[16] Its aim is frequently to 'transform the practitioners, the participants and the public's existing knowledge and experience'.[17] Furthermore, it is a place where opposite sides meet to 'affectively illuminate how truth collide rather to stake out oppositional claims or resolve binary conflicts'.[18] There are two important notions that theatre and peacebuilding studies share: conflict and the plurality of voices.

The format of the project was as follows: a group of thirty-two students aged twelve to fifteen (eight from each school), supported by eight teachers (two from each school), would meet once a week over a period of four months, each time at a different school, for two-hour-long theatre-based workshops. For most of the participants this was the first time they had set foot inside a Serbian or Muslim village, and the four-month duration of the project played an important part as longer periods of time allow people to create stronger personal relationships. To make sure the intermingling between different communities was achieved, a certain number of places in the different art groups were allocated to each school: the performing group, in charge of creating characters and *mise en scène*, comprised four young people from each school; the design group, comprising two students from each school, created set and costumes; while the music group, a small orchestra consisting of two students from each school, had the task of composing and performing the music for the piece; and the media group (two students from each school) used technology and social media to document and report on the process of making the theatre performance. The students had to collaborate within their particular groups as well as communicate across the groups for their ideas to be tested. This interaction supported the creation of an ensemble that broke through established ethnic divisions and allowed the young people to start forming friendships across socially imposed barriers. The role of the teachers and the Most Mira team was to initiate a creative environment, offer collaborative theatre-making skills and moderate conflict resolutions if needed. It is important to note that the schools themselves selected all the participants based on Most Mira's brief of eight students and two teachers per school and four different art strands. This meant the selected children were well-behaved and co-operative, and I assume came from families who were not strongly opposed to this type of project, meaning that the teachers and schools had no additional problems during the process.

Once a month, a British artist and I ran workshops in specific fields, such as music, movement and set design. Most Mira reports suggest that this collaboration with international guest artists was inspiring for all participants, students as well as teachers, as they brought different ideas and sensibilities about theatre-making not burdened or restricted by the local politics or traditional director-led approach.[19] This enabled participants to step out of their comfort zone and to open their minds to difference and diversity. For teachers this collaborative side of the process was different to the traditional hierarchical teacher-led educational system they operate in, and occasionally they struggled to permit students to make decisions. In their feedback, one of the teachers said: 'I particularly liked the creative freedom that the kids were given. That was completely different from what we are used to.'[20]

The show premiered at the local Prijedor Theatre and was then performed in all four schools and communities for a total of one thousand audience members. According to Humanity in Action:

> engaging young people acts as an important conduit for accessing adults who were less likely to participate in other reconciliation efforts, such as direct dialogue about overcoming differences and living together peacefully. Children's parents became stakeholders in youth reconciliation projects because they participated in many of their public activities such as performances or festivals. Working with youth thus serves the dual purpose of addressing the legacy of the conflict from the second generation's perspective, as well as including the war's victims and perpetrators in the conversation.[21]

Performing at the theatre was important not only because participants wanted to share their work with family and friends but also because it gave them a feelings of competence and accomplishment. The excitement and exhilaration experienced by the young people and their guests and parents at the theatre was extremely rewarding. 'Hey we were in the theatre!' and 'You would not believe it, my friend performed at the theatre!' were some of the exclamations given in the feedback.[22] School performances were not instantly welcomed: two principals attempted to cancel performances, but in the end I managed to renegotiate these decisions.

The two productions that formed *Shakespeare's Comedies* project were *San latnje noci* (*A Midsummer Night's Dream*) in 2013 and *Ludine price* (*Fool's Stories*) in 2014. Neither of the shows explicitly addressed interethnic conflict and segregation although this was implied, primarily as the theatre project was run by Most Mira, a peacebuilding organization rather than an international theatre company. Shakespeare was a natural choice as an international classic whose cultural presence and legacy extends beyond narrow bounds of nationalities and particular cultures, as well as across ages. In Bosnia and Herzegovina, *Hamlet* and *Romeo and Juliet* are included in the secondary school curriculum and Shakespeare's plays have formed an important part of the theatre repertoire across the region from the nineteenth century to the present day.[23] In post-conflict societies stories need to be chosen with extreme care and sensitivity, as they can deepen divisions instead of bridging them, especially in communities where myths and (mis)understandings of historical and cultural narratives are often used to create and perpetuate conflict. A number of practitioners working in post-war setups have emphasized the benefits of fictional narratives as opposed to documentary theatre practice. As James Thompson observes, the 'act of telling is not neutral but intertwined with multiple acts of narrative creation'.[24] Helen Nicholson argues that participants will find analogies with their own experience even if they are dealing with non-autobiographical narratives, as self and otherness are interrelated and implanted in the narrative. She proposes that the distinction between fiction and reality should be deliberately blurred in order to provide a safe space for 'participants to transform experience into dramatic metaphor.'[25] Thompson similarly points out that in some situations mutual understanding between divided communities is possible if the stories remain fictional and the work does not touch on the specific events as the 'real story required positions to be stated',[26] which can silence the conversation and disrupt the trust created between members of the opposing groups. As Dragan Klaić notes, 'the theatre of crisis, be it war, hunger, epidemics or civil unrest, can make sense if the artists focus not on the unfolding tragedy itself but on the ways it is being presented, reported, perceived and metaphorized by other dominant discourses.'[27]

By choosing Shakespeare's work, and his comedies in particular, as the starting point of our theatrical exploration, we could speak about the concerns of post-war reconciliation in an indirect way. They could be an instrument of enquiry into the construction of identity, and offer a critical insight into how to restore broken relationships through a change in attitude. Besides, the notion of having a comedy at the centre of our proposal helped Most Mira to engage people who would otherwise be reluctant to participate in such activities: it was a way to gain the trust of the schools and get them to participate in the project; to obtain all the Ministry of Education permits required to run the project in the first place; and to bring audiences to the theatre in large numbers.

A Midsummer Night's Dream was chosen because it includes the challenges of repairing broken relationships and of transforming disorder into the order. During the initial discussion about the play, what immediately interested the group was the rivalry between Titania and Oberon that affects the lives of mortals, the playfulness of the mischief-maker Puck, and, in what provided the production's opening, the metatheatricality of the Mechanicals' scenes. In Most Mira's final adaptation, the performance began with the Mechanicals getting ready for the rehearsal.[28] One of the actors is late and the rest of the group is waiting uncomfortably on stage, apologetically smiling and shrugging at the audience, frantically whispering something to each other and surreptitiously checking the backstage area. The ambiguity as to whether this was or was not a part of the performance gradually elicited audience laughter. When the late-arriving actor playing Nick Bottom finally stormed on, the play proper began, occasionally still playing with the multi-layered reality by maintaining direct communication with the audience:

DUNJA
> Je l' celo društvance na gomili?

VRATILO
> Najbolje bi bilo da se svi prozovemo – jedan po jedan, prema ulogama.

GLADNICA
> Al' pre svega, Dunjo, da nam kažeš šta taj komad uopšte tretira; pa onda imenuj glumce, i zatim pređi na stvar.[24]

QUINCE
> Marry, our play is, The most lamentable comedy, and most cruel death of Pyramus and Thisbe.

BOTTOM
> A very good piece of work, I assure you, and a
> merry one.   (1.2.10–13)

This opening, where actors directly addressed the audience and presented the notion of 'lamentable comedy' and 'most cruel death' to the audience, not only immediately exposed and subverted the notions of reality and mimesis but likewise those of comedy and tragedy.

A year later, *Fools' Stories* played further with the ideas of comedy and jeering in relation to misfortune, when the character of a Fool takes the audience on a journey across the globe to show stories depicting 'what fools these mortals be!' (3.2.116). The text was an adaptation of *The Tempest* and *King Lear*, interlinked with the bricolage of Fool's lines gathered from across Shakespeare's opus. This production also embraced metatheatrical elements and the performance began with house lights still on and a joyful Fool wandering on the stage, casually chatting to the audience, whishing them good day, asking how they are or commenting on the space, waving to his friends or relatives in the audience and then suddenly bumping into a group of actors entering the stage. This knock was a cue for the auditorium lights to dim down and stage lights to go on:

> ACTOR 1
> How now! What art thou?
> FOOL
> A man, sir.
> ACTOR 2
> What dost thou profess? What wouldst thou with us?
> FOOL
> I do profess to be no less than I seem; to serve
> him truly that will put me in trust: to love him
> that is honest; to converse with him that is wise,
> and says little; to fear judgment; to fight when I
> cannot choose; and to eat no fish.
> (*King Lear*, 1.4.10–13)

At the end of this initial encounter between a group of actors and a Fool, which used Kent's and Lear's lines from *King Lear* but placed them in a different context of as the beginning of Fool's stories. Fools offers to take us on a journey 'Let me be your guide for today.' [2*] He and the actors steer us into the storm that opens *The Tempest* and the house lights go down, uncovering the magical world of the play.

The disruption of theatre conventions was a great source of laughter for the audience and freed up the performers. The character of the wise Fool and his counterpart, trickster Puck, were developed as sharp-witted figures who were licensed to tell the truth, cross borders and float in between realities. Apart from the music and choreography this quality was portrayed on stage through 'frozen scenes' where Puck or Ariel would 'stop the time' and manipulate other characters on stage by placing them in different positions, desirable states or swapping their costumes creating confusion and bemusement. This quality of, as Tim Prentki puts it, 'conveying a sense of the world in flux' provided a valuable source of amusement and playfulness; the Fool is a 'figure of fluidity and insinuation, at once nowhere and everywhere, intrinsically at odds with the classical canon of separation and decorum.'[30] Disjointedness is in the essence of the Fool's identity; it balances wit and foolishness while revealing stories, events and actions, interpreting human nature, underlining the absurdities of certain actions and illuminating the social order we accept or not.

The exploration of *The Tempest* brought out the themes of right and wrong, justice and redemption. However, the division of right and wrong is not simple and straightforward as the character of Prospero is a victim of his brother's wrongdoing but also an oppressor of Caliban and Ariel. Prospero's manipulation of, or withholding of information about, his and his daughter's past, and the ending of the play, when the second generation shows compassion and bring reconciliation and love, powerfully resonate with the Bosnian predicament around the war narrative.

The next journey the Fool and actors take us on is a tale of an old king who one day decided to divide his kingdom among his three daughters. Once again, the audience could draw a strong parallel between the division of the kingdom and that of Bosnia's destructive struggle for political power, and the dishonesty that penetrates the political sphere. But this reworking of the story has a happy ending. The pivotal dramatic moment is a scene of a great thunderstorm when Lear and Fool are looking for shelter and having an argument about being a fool:

FOOL
    Dost thou know the difference, my boy, between
    a bitter fool and a sweet fool?
KING LEAR
    No, lad; teach me.
FOOL
    That lord that counselled thee
    To give away thy land,
    Come place him here by me,
    Do thou for him stand:
    The sweet and bitter fool
    Will presently appear;
    The one in motley here,
    The other found out there.
KING LEAR
    Dost thou call me fool, boy?
FOOL
    All thy other titles thou hast given away; that thou
    was born with.
    (1.4.132–144)

The storm gets stronger, as does Lear's rage and his unwillingness to admit his mistakes and perceive the truth. During the storm, Cordelia finds the ragged and disorientated Lear wandering around with his Fool and rescue them. Lear is overwhelmed with remorse and ready to see the truth, admits his wrongdoing and asks for forgiveness. The king and his daughter reconcile and this Fool's story ends with a great celebration party and a notion that

> All the world's a stage,
> And all the men and women merely players:
> They have their exits and their entrances;
> And one man in his time plays many parts.
> (*As You Like It*, 2.7.140–143)

This fortunate resolution of the plays is important. Comedy storylines often draw us into the dark and tragic world of misfortune where injustice is done and characters suffer trouble. As Matthew Bevis puts it, 'comedy does not preclude tragedy; it presupposes it'; however, the fortunate resolutions turns the tragic story into a comedy, 'a story in which people *can* believe their luck.'[31] The purpose of a happy ending is not merely to offer a 'feel-good' effect in contrast with the grim reality, but rather to call to action and to envisage a better future. As Prentki puts it, 'getting life going again is one of the key social functions of the fool and trickster. His is an art of survival, not of tragedy.'[32]

This notion of survival through folly could correspond with Thompson's advocacy of *affect* instead of *effect* as the main focus of applied theatre practices in war and post war settings. Thompson understands affect as 'the bodily sensation that is provoked particularly by aesthetic experiences... the force that emerges from attention to pleasure, astonishment, joy and beauty.'[33] This alteration was inspired by years of experience of working in conflict zones (particularly Sri Lanka and Rwanda), and specifically by an incident that occurred in a rehabilitation centre for child soldiers with whom Thompson ran a theatre project, where twenty-seven boys were killed, apparently (it was never officially confirmed) by local residents. He observes that applied theatre practice, concentrated too much on the 'identifiable social or educational impact', can become limited and ineffective. Additionally, he points out that 'by failing to recognize affect – bodily responses, sensations and aesthetic pleasures – much of the power of performance can be missed.'[34] He correspondingly advocates for the 'theatre of relief' to be recognised as important in the zones of conflict and not to be discredited as trivial entertainment.[35] These notions of relief and *affect* can be linked not only with the relief theory of humour as the venting the nervous energy and release of tension in stressed or dangerous situations,[36] but also with William Demastes' contention that comedy has the power to change. Starting from the view that the mind is embodied and drawing from neuroscience, biology and psychology he concludes that:

> Comedy creates an environment that can encourage our consciousnesses to comprehend and adapt to the wisdom enigmatically expressed by our unconsciousnesses. Through comic exposure – and perhaps unawares – we become more understanding of the other we've previously excluded, whether it is previously *othered* ideas, peoples, or cultures.[37]

More recently, literature has emerged that offers interesting insight into the function of humour during the war and violence, from the Holocaust to the Sarajevo siege and the current Syrian war, that challenges this binary between 'high serious art' and 'low entertainment' and pointing out that jokes, comedy and laughter are survival mechanisms as well as a form of resistance.[38] Analysing the function of humour during genocide Üngör and Verkerke concluded that:

> the fact that people joked about the hardships, their oppressors and themselves, demonstrates that victims are not that passive at all. They were fundamentally aware of what was going on, commented on it with jokes and coped with it through humour. This testifies to the resilience of the survivors. After their victimization, humour could still function as a coping, cohesive and critical mechanism. Cracking jokes when living circumstances are dire was a way of maintaining human dignity.[39]

These strands encapsulate many important aspects of the practice that I am discussing: the (unavoidable) political aspects of theatre practice in the context of peacebuilding; the ethics, in particular shunning explicit narratives about the war; and the aesthetic of the practice that emphasises comedy and playfulness.

The theatre arts contribute to the reconciliation process in Bosnia and Herzegovina on the community level in a variety of ways. Some projects are process-oriented and serve the purposes of therapy or healing for individuals and communities. Others are product-oriented, aiming to educate and tell a story to wider audiences about different aspects of the conflict. The value of theatre within the post-conflict context lies in its potential to challenge, construct and deconstruct different narratives while offering space for multiple positions without enforcing the pretention that conflict should be resolved.

Most Mira's approach is to use 'art that humanises'[40] by focusing on ensemble performance and a collaborative model of theatre-making. This creative approach aims to encourage understanding between young people from different backgrounds and to strengthen their connections and possible friendships. The basic working method was to start each workshop with fun warm-up exercises for the whole group that support team work (such as the 'Yes, and' game, 'Word at a time story' and 'Zip-Zap-Boing'). Next the groups worked on their own tasks or two groups collaborated if they were working on a particular scene (for example, if the scene incorporates music with movement). Everyone met for a snack break and at the end of the workshop this was followed by a collective debrief at the end of the day.

While theatre can certainly serve as a good platform for political debate, it was clear from the responses to the questionnaires at the beginning of the project that the main expectations of the participants were to meet new people, learn new skills and have a good time. At the same time (apart from the fear that they would forget their lines), several participants raised concerns about the project failing and the possibility of negativity or abusiveness from other participants. One participant said: 'I do not like people that are in a dark mood and I also do not like when someone is offending people that I love'. In the final report it was observed that: 'young people displayed some of the divisive behaviour that we observed in adults, but were very quick to move on for the sake of having fun.'[41]

A Midsummer Night's Dream premiered at the theatre with great success and the 'impressions poster' was covered with positive feedback from the audience. However, when it was performed in Kozarac school, the performance was disrupted by the heckling and derision from older pupils. I was on the verge of stopping the performance, not only because the comments were distracting but also because I was concerned that the ensemble might disintegrate, and I was unsure which side the participants from Kozarac school would take. But then the ensemble stood up together and in a humorous manner started addressing themselves directly to the disruptive group until it eventually fell silent. After the performance the group was very excited and proud of how they had managed to handle the situation. For me personally, that was a positive indicator that the ethnic identity was at least for the duration of the project overruled by the strong feeling of belonging to this theatre project.

There is no set recipe for making theatre in the context of postwar peacebuilding, but using Shakespearean comedy worked in this particular situation, where clashing narratives and distrust of others prevent dialogue and deepen social division. It worked as a welcoming invite to the theatrical journey. The *Shakespeare's Comedies* project did not address the war directly and it did not provide a space for telling stories about the recent past, but it directly countered the forced separation and dehumanization of the other by allowing a space in which young people could create their own value systems based upon their experience and not upon inherited beliefs. It would be too idealistic (if not foolish) to say that this creative experience has the potential to single-handedly oppose single-minded narratives. However, it can help its participants to untangle their presumptions and thus perhaps allow them to cross boundaries and appreciate multiple perspectives. Hopefully it will contribute to the process of recognising a shared humanity beyond ethnic identities.

> KENT
> Who's there?
> FOOL
> ... that's a wise man and a fool.
> (*King Lear*, 3.2.39–41)

Maja Milatović-Ovadia is a freelance theatre director, drama lecturer and PhD researcher at the Royal School of Speech and Drama. Her research interests include the use of humour and comedy within applied theatre practice in post-conflict settings. Since 2009 she has been actively involved with Most Mira, a charity organisation that uses art to support the process of reconciliation in Bosnia and Herzegovina. Originally from former Yugoslavia, she is currently based in London.

Notes

1. The other three camps in the Prijedor area were Keratem, Manjaca and Trnopolje.
2. In 1992 Ed Vulliamy, a *Guardian* journalist, Penny Marshall, a reporter for Independent Television News (ITN), and Ian Williams, a *Channel 4 News* reporter gained access to the Omarska and Trnopolje camp.
3. Significantly, during the trials a tthe International Crime Tribunal for Former Yugoslavia rape (of women as well as men) was qualified as a form of torture and recognized as a crime against humanity and a tool for committing genocide, for the first time in the history of this court. http://www.icty.org/en/features/crimes-sexual-violence/landmark-cases.
4. Roberto Belloni, 'Bosnia: Dayton is Dead! Long Live Dayton!', *Nationalism & Ethnic Politics*, 15, no. 3–4: 355–75. https://doi.org/10.1080/13537110903372367.
5. Bosnia and Herzegovina is one of the seven newly-formed countries that came out of the fallout of Yugoslavia. Its political configuration is complicated. According to the Dayton Accord the country is divided into two entities – Federation (where Bosniaks and Croats constitute the ethnic majority) and Republic Srpska (with Serbs as the ethnic majority) and Brcko District. Another level of political division are the cantons (ten of them) and then municipalities (63 in Republic Srpska and 74 in the Federation). The head of State is a three-member body that serves collectively (Serb, Croat, Muslim).
6. Belloni, 'Bosnia: Dayton is Dead!'
7. Martina Fischer and Ljubinka Petrovic-Zimer (eds) *Berghof Report No. 18, Dealing With a Past in the Wester Balkans, Initiatives for Peacebuilding and Transitional Justice in Bosnia- Herzegovina, Serbia and Croatia* (Berlin: Berghof Foundation, 2013). http://www.berghof-foundation.org/fileadmin/redaktion/ Publications/ Papers/Reports/br18e.pdf/ (Accessed 7 December 2016). Edina Becirevic, 'The Issue of Genocidal Intent and Denial of Genocide: A Case Study of Bosnia and Herzegovina', *East European Politics and Societies*, 4 (2010), 480–502. Dubravka Stojanovic, 'Construction of Historical Consciousness: The Case of Serbian History Textbooks', in Maria Todorova (ed.), *Balkan Identities: Nation and Memory*, (London: Hurst and Company, 2004), 327–338.
8. Transparency International, https://www.transparency.org/country/BIH (Accessed 27 September 2018). Danijel Kovacevic, 'Half of All Bosnians Live Outside Bosnia', *Balkan Insight*, 8 August 2017, http://www.balkaninsight.com/en/article/half-of-all-bosnians-live-outside-bosnia-08-07-2017, accessed 14 September 2018).
9. Daniel Bar-Tal and Gemma Bennink, 'The nature of reconciliation as an outcome and as a process', Yaacov Bar-Siman-Tov (ed.), *From conflict Resolution to Reconciliation,* (Oxford: Oxford University Press, 2004), 26.
10. Lina Strupinskienė, 'What is reconciliation and are we there yet?': Different types and levels of reconciliation: A case study of Bosnia and Herzegovina', *Journal of Human Rights*, 4 (2016), 452–72.
11. See John Paul Lederach, *Building peace: sustainable reconciliation in divided societies* (Washington: United States Institute of Peace Press, 1997); Denise J. D. Sandole and Hugo van der Merwe (eds.), *Conflict Resolution Theory and Practice: Integration and Application* (Manchester: Manchester University Press, 1993).

12. For a week local young people (around 400 each year) participated in art, drama, music, dance, circus skills and journalism workshops run by international volunteers (artists, academics, activists). At the end of the week they performed and showcased their work for their parents, friends and community.
13. For more about Most Mira's work see www.mostmiraproject.com.
14. In spring 2009 I was meeting Zrikna Bralo, a friend of mine originally from Sarajevo living in London for a coffee before we went to see a movie at the National Film Theatre. She was involved with setting up a small charity that would work with youth in Bosnia using art to support peacebuilding. They were preparing its first project, a week-long festival for 250 young people. Operating on very tight funding she was looking for volunteers. I volunteered and for ten years I was going back.
15. The majority of the students had not had any experience of acting and performing. Drama is not a part of the school curriculum and in some schools it is offered once a year as part of extracurricular activities.
16. See Sonja Arsham Kuftinec, *Theatre, Facilitation, and Nation Formation in the Balkans and Middle East* (London: Palgrave Macmillan 2009); Guglielmo Schinina, 'Here We Are: Social Theatre and Some Open Questions about Its Development', *TDR: The Drama Review*, 48:3 (2004), 17–31); James Thompson, 'Ugly, Unglamorous and Dirty: Theatre of relief/reconciliation/liberation in places of war', *Research in Drama Education: The Journal of Applied Theatre and Performance*, 7:1 (2002), 108–14.; James Thompson and Richard Schechner, 'Why "Social Theatre"?', *TDR: The Drama Review*, 48: 3 (2004); Craig Zelizer, 'The Role of Artistic Processes in Peace-Building in Bosnia-Herzegovina', *Peace and Conflict Studies*, 10:2 (2003), 62–76.
17. Thompson and Schechner, 'Why "Social Theatre"?'
18. Sonja Arsham Kuftinec, *Theatre, Facilitation, and Nation Formation in the Balkans and Middle East* (Palgrave Macmillan 2009), xiv.
19. Most Mira Reports 2011, 2012, 2013 (accessed via https://www.mostmiraproject.org/blank)
20. Most Mira Project feedback, 2013.
21. Humanity in Action, 'Engaging youth in peacebuilding through art in Bosnia and Herzegovina' (Report 2013). https://projectonpeacebuilding.wordpress.com/2014/05/20/2013-report-creative-commons-engaging-youth-in-peacebuilding-through-art-in-bosnia-and-herzegovina, accessed 25 October 2018.
22. Ibid.
23. The first translator of Shakespeare's work in the Serbian language was Dr. Laza Kostić (1841–1910). He was an eminent intellectual, lawyer, poet, polyglot and thinker of nineteen century.
24. James Thompson, *Digging Up Stories*, (Manchester: Manchester University Press, 2005), 25.
25. Helen Nicholson, *Applied Drama* (Palgrave Macmillan, 2005), 66.
26. Thompson, 'Ugly, Unglamorous and Dirty', 111.
27. Thompson, *Digging Up Stories*, 26.
28. The final text of the performance used the translations by Velimir Živojinić, *Vilijam Sekspir, Sabrana Dela* (Beograd: Zavod za ubženike Beograd, 2011). Scenes and lines were cut and rearranged in different contexts. For example, the

dialogue between a Kent and Lear was used as an opening of the Fool's story as a dialogue between Fool and a group of actors.
29. Final script of the Most Mira adaptation *Fool's Stories*.
30. Tim Prentki, *The Fool in European Theatre* (Basingstoke: Palgrave, 2012), 5. 121.
31. Matthew Bevis, *Comedy: A Very Short Introduction.* (Oxford: Oxford University Press, 2013), 53.
32. Prentki, *The Fool in European Theatre*, 4.
33. James Thompson, *Performance Affects: Applied Theatre and the End of Effect* (Basingstoke: Palgrave, 2009), 135.
34. ibid. 7.
35. James Thompson, 'Ugly, Unglamorous and Dirty', 111
36. See John Morreall, *The Philosophy of Laughter and Humor*, (New York: State University of New York Press, 1987). James Palmer, *Taking Humour Seriously*, (Routledge 1994).
37. William W. Demastes, *Comedy Matters, from Shakespeare to Stoppard*, (Palgrave Macmillan, 2008), 180.
38. See Patrick Duggan and Lisa Peschel (eds), *Performing (for) Survival* (London: Palgrave Macmillan, 2015); Ugur Umit Üngör and Valerie Amandine Verkerke, 'Funny as hell: The function of humour during and after genocide', *European Journal of Humour Research* (2015), 80–101, https://www.europeanjournalofhumour.org/index. php/ejhr/article/view/119/. Davor Diklić, *Teatar u ratnom Sarajevu 1992–1995* (Sarajevo-Zemun: Biblioteka Manhattan, 2004), Louise Peacock, 'Sending laughter around the world', *Humor-International Journal of Humor Research*, 29:2 (2015), 223–41.
39. Üngör and Verkerke, 'Funny as hell', 97.
40. Humanity in Action, 'Engaging youth in peacebuilding through art in Bosnia and Herzegovina', (Report 2013), [Consulted at https://projectonpeacebuilding .wordpress.com/2014/05/20/2013-report-creative-commons-engaging-youth-in -peacebuilding-through-art-in-bosnia-and-herzegovina 25. October 2018)
41. Most Mira, Report 2013.

Chapter 4
Getting It on Its Feet
Exploring The Politics and Processes of Shakespeare Outside the Traditional Classroom

Karl Falconer

The actor Benedict Cumberbatch, speaking at the South Bank Arts Awards in 2018, advocated greater class diversity in the theatre, whilst thanking his Harrow School teachers for fostering his own talent in drama.[1] Sir Patrick Stewart, meanwhile, the child of a working-class Yorkshire family, talked elsewhere of his hometown's investment in local drama projects as being an obvious bridge to his own professional career.[2] For Stewart, an early engagement with participatory arts, outside of the classroom, helped to develop a passion for Shakespeare that was deemed a curriculum necessity in Cumberbatch's private schooling system. In current education structures, as specified by the National Curriculum in England, Shakespeare may not enter a child's life until the final quarter of their compulsory education. Do we need, then, to look beyond the classroom for those opportunities that allow us to develop a deeper

Notes for this section begin on page 66.

relationship with the work? With the current offering being critiqued amid worries that 'pupils can leave school without studying anything more than bite-sized extracts of Shakespeare's most famous plays', the alternative realm of participatory education may hold the key, especially for working-class students, where, 'social class remains the strongest predictor of educational achievement in the UK.'[3] Whilst a knowledge of Shakespeare is not a critical life skill, withholding a more meaningful relationship with his work may both deprive future learners of language skills, and reduce access to a shared understanding of Britain's most widespread cultural export. Reducing the number of playscripts in the classroom, in favour of the novel, additionally removes a gifted opportunity for oral demonstration, vital for public speaking and presentational confidence.

In this chapter, I will discuss the findings from my own company's history of performing Shakespeare with young people, as well as a number of workshops conducted with the specific aim of identifying and exploring potential barriers to engagement amongst working-class groups, and seeing how exploring Shakespeare outside of a classroom setting can help to overcome them. The contextual framework of this study takes me away from the classroom and into what David Greunewald calls the 'social construction' of space beyond the mainstream.[4] I will explore the relationship between class and space, to understand how we can use the concept of the safe space to neutralise and de-politicise education, both for current students and for those left uninspired by their own educational experiences under very different governments and educational agendas.

In the action research model, I believe it important to contextualise one's own experience. I identify as working-class and found my own early experience of Shakespeare to be without meaningful links to my own life. Thanks to the Shakespeare Schools Festival, an introduction to Shakespeare's plays, through practical drama activities and performance, began a slow process of understanding and enjoying his work in performance, which, in turn, helped to shape the founding values of my theatre company, PurpleCoat.[5] Based in Liverpool, our work took on a classical focus, driven by the social aims of encouraging a relationship with Shakespeare formed on one's own terms, by staging productions that combined strong visuals with a focus on foregrounding regional identity. This developed, through an Arts Council-funded Young Actors' company, into a body of work that aimed to make Shakespeare more relevant to a local working-class audience. I am from the same background as the people I make work with and for. My position, in being able to create my own company's mission and values, rather than working for another pre-existing organization with its own legacy, compromises and history, separates me from the 'extant practice architectures' of 'facilitators external to the community,' where the results of analysis may be, 'at odds with local responses.'[6] PurpleCoat is a theatre company founded by myself to facilitate alternative approaches to Shakespeare in production, primarily through a working-class lens. Our work seeks to work with the audience we have, based in Liverpool, England, to reimagine what his work can look like for a 21st century working-class audience and creator. Having faced the same barriers to engaging with Shakespeare and finding his language confusing, I believe that my own experience can model a potential journey for others from my community, where I aim to demonstrate that socio-economic circumstance need not be a barrier to enjoying his work.

Figures recorded between 2010 and 2021 point to declines of 38% at GCSE and 31% at A-Level for arts-based qualifications.[7] Combined with the ending (announced in August 2018) of the flagship Travelex discount ticket scheme at London's National Theatre, the pedagogic disciplines of drama and literature face a challenge to justify the continued relevance of Shakespeare in an ever-changing landscape.[8] Further evidence of Shakespeare's vulnerability to public opinion is expressed in the findings of a report commissioned by the Royal Shakespeare Company in 2019, where 80% of Year 10 students claimed that 'Shakespeare has no relevance to their lives.'[9] The existential threat posed to the entire theatre industry in the wake of the Covid-19 pandemic has added new pressure for all theatre forms to justify to their audiences the investment of time and resources required, at a time when theatre attendance and mass-gatherings are down across the board, as audiences continue to stay away in the face of perceived health risks.[10] Against the immense rise in popularity of streaming services, the general shift to flexible working-patterns and the continued economic and social fallout of the 'new normal', the case for all theatre to persuade an audience to attend becomes more precarious than ever before.

Traditionally, the work of Shakespeare has been perceived, as being, 'socially inappropriate for certain classes of performer.'[11] At a time when theatre programming is aiming to meet the challenge of audience numbers and diversity, in which traditional structures and patterns of programming are seen as being indicative of a theatre, 'stuck in the 20th century', the intentions and audiences for a potential Shakespeare booking are likely to shift and change.[12] It is crucial for theatre-makers to allow Shakespeare's image to continually develop through a constant renegotiation with the work, where re-interpretation comes from diverse cultural appropriation, not least because innovative programming has provided demonstrably positive results. London's Donmar Warehouse all-female Shakespeare trilogy, the Young Vic's musical adaptation of *Twelfth Night* and the Everyman Rep-Company's *Othello* are recent notable productions that have renegotiated perceived norms of Shakespeare with critical and box-office success.[13] While the image of Shakespeare, as Sandeep Purewal suggests, has been singularly designed in the past, as a symbol of 'Britain's ideological superiority,' we appear to be in a period of transition, where perceptions of gender, race and class are open for new interpretation.[14]

Andrew Murphy has demonstrated, in *Shakespeare for the People*, that Shakespeare has been interlinked with class culture for over 150 years.[15] Murphy references an article from *Reynold's Newspaper*, which reports on the crowd of 10,000 working-class citizens of London who pulled together in celebration of the tercentenary of Shakespeare's birth.[16] Without their efforts, following the 'blunders and failures' of the officially planned celebration, 'there would have been no London commemoration at all!' This moment makes clear, as Murphy reminds us, that 'Shakespeare had become entwined with issues of class by the middle decades of the nineteenth century.'[17] Who had the right to his ownership was already a pertinent question, and the events of the tercentenary procession at Primrose Hill highlighted 'the extent to which the working class really had taken possession of Shakespeare.'[18]

Over 150 years later, in 1997, Prime Minister Tony Blair and Deputy PM John Prescott naively prophesied the end of working-class life.[19] In 2013, a BBC report followed the thread of New Labour's neoliberal vision, with its Great British Class Calculator declaring that, 'traditional British social divisions of upper, middle and working-class seem out of date in the 21st century.'[20] For some, the rigidity of systems such as formal education points to their role in 'establishing and maintaining class distinction.'[21] Education has a significant part to play in undermining and re-establishing class, gender and racial definition. Scarborough-born theatre director Nick Bagnall, associate director of the Liverpool Everyman, has spoken of his school education of Shakespeare as, 'the most boring experience of my life. I remember thinking, I hate this Shakespeare, because of the way it was taught to me.' For Bagnall, the experience of, 'this crap teacher [starting] to read *Macbeth*...' nearly extinguished an interest in Shakespeare, which was only reignited after a trip to the theatre. 'After that, I realised that it wasn't just tights and ruffs, it could be inventive, imaginative and really bold and sexy.'[22] David Kolb developed the idea of the learning cycle and highlighted the importance of reflection in developing future practice.[23] We must err on the side of caution, however, when using any singular narrative to articulate a community-wide experience. The work of the French theorist and philosopher Jacques Rancière, summaried by Sian Adiseshiah as 'unintentionally reinforcing the disempowerment of working-class agency through establishing the working-class subject as disempowered'[24] gets to the heart of this complexity. To assume that inequality is consistently widespread is to fail to address the complexity of the issue, and contested definitions of class only make generalisations of experience or development harder. We must therefore account for the individual whilst recognizing the potential and limitation of scope to draw wider analysis.

The Short View

In 2018 I conducted a number of workshops with Meladrama, a company in the outskirts of Manchester working to 'instigate social change', in the North West of England.[25] The aim of these sessions, with three groups of twenty participants aged 6–11, 12–18 and 18+, was to explore the short-term impact of active rehearsal techniques, outside the classroom, upon perceptions of the participants' relationship with Shakespeare. Participants self-defined as working-class and were categorised by the company's managing director as being 'turned off' by Shakespeare. The sessions were deeply indebted to the work of Joe Winston and Miles Tandy, whose practical rehearsal techniques, which introduce language gradually, through play, were used throughout.[26] Both the teenage and adult groups were invited to complete an online questionnaire after their workshops, to better collect their thoughts and to measure any change in their attitudes towards the work.

A series of questions were provided, with a numerical scale, for participants to rate their responses. In each, 1 was the lowest or most negative value, and 10 was the highest. Questions attempted to measure the change in attitude towards engaging with Shakespeare through live attendance at a performance, reading or performing in his plays. Participants were asked to complete questionnaires before and after the workshop, to evidence what, if any, change had taken place. Every single respondent, in the teenage group, recorded higher scores 'after' than 'before.' One participant reported a rise from 3 to 8, when asked to consider their overarching impression of Shakespeare's work. When considering Shakespeare's perceived relevance, results varied. One student began at 8 and stayed at 8, whilst others jumped from 3 to 9. The lowest increases were from 1 to 2 and 1 to 4, which are still poor overall, despite the increase. When asked to measure the likelihood of watching Shakespeare, the responses were equally varied, with several students reporting high likelihoods of 8 or 9, and a few reporting scores as low as 2 and 3.

Students were asked to summarise their initial impression towards Shakespeare and to explain where they believe this originated. One student suggested that impressions are formed because, 'people... have to do Shakespeare.' Multiple students reported their initial impression of Shakespeare as being, 'complicated and boring', with some explanation given, including 'the way it is portrayed by the media,' with one student saying that they 'didn't get a good first impression, the language is very different.' Another student expanded, 'I think for teenagers like myself, Shakespeare is something that you're nervous to throw yourself into... many young people dismiss his writing and jump to the easy option of saying that they don't understand.' Another accounted for their negative impression as simply 'because of school.' When specifically asking students how the workshop was different from school, they reported that, 'it made me understand more.' One student focused on the practical element of the workshop, mentioning how it made them, 'see Shakespeare in a different light. It made me less reluctant to study his works.' Another wrote of how 'the workshop was refreshing, I now see Shakespeare as being accessible and not just for special drama schools in London.'

When asked to consider what elements of the workshop helped, specifically, to engender a positive response to Shakespeare, replies included 'the context,' 'understanding the words a bit more,' 'feeling the emotion in my body,' and 'the practical elements.' However, when asked to highlight anything that wasn't enjoyed, or which created a negative impression of Shakespeare, one student returned again to 'reading the words.' When asked if they would enjoy rehearsing an entire Shakespeare play, using the same approach, the same student continued 'not particularly, because ... I don't like the language and I will probably stutter.' None of the students had a medical stutter, and this comment points towards wider issues of confidence amongst students which I consider below.

The Long View

In 2018, I invited alumni of the PurpleCoat Young Actors Company to complete a similar questionnaire, in order to consider the way in which the relationship between participant and Shakespeare is perceived, longer term. Respondents claimed that an active approach, outside the classroom, was 'engaging and easier to understand', with all respondents reporting that their understanding of the play, the language, and contextual history of the playwright increased. Our Young Actors Company was an extra-curricular opportunity for students, who joined us through external application processes not connected to schools. We recruited some of these young people through school workshops, while the work itself was rehearsed in a variety of community halls around the city centre. Young people could stay with us until the age of 18, and in the manner of many such voluntary participation, some would return for several performances whilst others would join intermittently, as life, education, finance and general interest changed. Our work primarily involved the staging of Elizabethan drama, although this was often done within a larger wraparound program of skills development and actor training. In progressing to alumni status, participants had left to study at drama school or to continue an engagement through our adult programs or involvement in alternative provision elsewhere.

Alumni discussed with us the way in which our workshop focus on the context of the gunpowder plot in relation to *Macbeth,* as one example, helped them to appreciate some of Shakespeare's many contemporary references and relation to his wider world. In this way, respondents appeared to be able to better articulate how Shakespeare was a contemporary writer in his own time, responding to the concerns and events of his own age, and drawing parallels to how writers create work now. Every respondent reported that they had been to watch more Shakespeare since working with us, although this overlooks their predisposition to attend the theatre in the first place. Although participants were recruited on the basis of their socio-economic status, the mere fact that they were compelled or encouraged to attend auditions and rehearsals perhaps creates a further distinction of aspiration within the category we collectively describe as working-class. This opens up wider questions about whether the students we worked with would have found other opportunities in absence of our own, and asks us to consider who we were still not engaging through our selection processes. Whether an engagement in theatre and Shakespeare is, by definition, aspirational, and whether that places our work within a meritocratic framework is a question PurpleCoat and all theatre-makers must wrestle with to discover the true purpose of our intervention.

When asked if they can remember any of the active rehearsal techniques all students had a reply. This is particularly positive, as it had been between two to five years since many of these participants had been in rehearsal with us. Among the techniques remembered were a focus on 'breathing because you need to get the words out without sounding breathless', 'walking in character', 'the cast mirroring our role', and 'creating shapes physically with our bodies.' It is worth noting, that without any prompting, all students recounted physical activities and nothing specifically text-based, raising the legitimate question of whether engagement was developed with the exercises themselves or with Shakespeare specifically. These same exercises could have prompted increased engagement with other classical or contemporary writers in the same way, making the choice of pedagogy the achievement here and not an eye-opening renegotiation with Shakespeare. This is a question which requires further study and modelling from researchers more broadly, but we must also interrogate whether this matters, or whether a change is enthusiasm is enough regardless of how we got there. When asked if Shakespeare continues to impact their lives today, students replied that 'I want to perform a lot more classical theatre', that 'Shakespeare is now my favourite writer', and that they can see how 'social issues that were around in the 16th and 17th centuries are still around today.'

The feedback of the alumni clearly demonstrates long-term memories of a physically focused, extra-curricular rehearsal process, and they articulate compelling evidence of its continued impact.

Almost all characteristics of the relationship with Shakespeare are expressed positively, although it is problematic to assume this as an end product for all. The conditioning of an activity outside of formal education helped in avoiding the lack of autonomy afforded by curriculum, where John Dewey highlights how, 'the child must do these things for the sake of something else he [sic] is to do.'[27] This is something evident in the teenage group at Meladrama, where high-school students were, initially at least, most visibly resistant to attempting to renegotiate a relationship with Shakespeare. The experience of a guest facilitator coming into the group to explore Shakespeare was perhaps reminiscent and triggering of a school experience, which it took these teenagers longer to trust, in ways not necessarily reflected in the other age categories. Natasha Ryan, co-director of PurpleCoat's Young Actors company, summarised the benefit of an inclusive, participatory ethos. Reflecting on the fact that participation was voluntary and that costs were subsidised through Arts Council funding, Ryan remarked that 'it creates a safe space for people to take it at their own pace and to try out ideas, as opposed to following a rule book, which most young people are doing when they're preparing for exams. It is nice to explore it in a way that doesn't have constraints to it.'[28] The issue of the 'chasm in confidence' between middle- and working-class pupils, where 'growing up working-class erodes your confidence, almost by design,' is further exacerbated by the rise in social media and its effect on mental health.[29] This is one of the difficulties in measuring impact. We cannot rely solely on interviewing participants whilst barriers of confidence and ability to express oneself present obstacles to promoting growth. We must take inspiration, also, from transitive and flexible means; observing a participant's engagement and enjoyment, for example, although this needs to remain substantiated with robust measurement and analysis.

During one Meladrama workshop, one student told me, 'I can't speak [the text] because I don't know what an Elizabethan man sounded like and I don't sound like that.' In both the Meladrama workshops and the PurpleCoat Young Actors productions, participants were encouraged to use their own accents to unlock the language in a way that is meaningful to them. Voice coach Patsy Rodenburg links voice with confidence, declaring the implication of accent bias as being 'the right to speak is mine and mine alone.'[30] Encouraging the use of one's own voice can be a step towards appropriation that can address the issue of class confidence. In her 2012 study, 'I Need Help!', Jessica Calcaro found that 'children's social-class backgrounds affects when and how they seek help in the classroom.'[31] The initial reaction, in the workshop at Melodrama, for under-11s, was one of excitement at the idea of working with Shakespeare, gesturing towards the implication of cultural conditioning, rather than an inherent resistance to Shakespeare's text. At the same time, the case of the student worried about stuttering when speaking the text opens up a wider conversation, where assumed issues of engaging young people with classical work actually masks deeper inequalities around confidence and cultural capital. It is possible, therefore, that our concerns around a lack of engagement with Shakespeare is not to do with Shakespeare itself, but is a symptom of a deeper social and cultural root cause.

Class and confidence are intimately linked. Vik Loveday writes that 'the labelling of groups as 'hard to reach' arguably acts to produce certain groups as problematic.'[32] The same could be said of the stigmatisation of Shakespeare; it is not Shakespeare's work itself that is the problem, but wider issues of class confidence in an environment where, 'we are still educating different social classes for different functions in society.'[33] In effect, by labelling Shakespeare as difficult, a 'code' that can only be cracked with sustained effort, attention is directed away from the root cause of class instability, which may be more complicated for educators to resolve. The message appears to be that the problem of engaging with Shakespeare is assigned to the individual to solve, rather than the society responsible for enabling the inequality in the first place. If these negative impressions are not addressed as we progress from school into adult life, it is argued that disadvantaged groups, 'abandon the very aspiration to question or change their lot in life.'[34]

Aspiration may, perhaps, be the key. The PurpleCoat Young Actors Company staged full-length productions, which were often presented at the Royal Shakespeare Company's outdoor performance space, The Dell, as a part of their Open Stages programme for amateur theatre companies. 'I think aspiration was really important', Ryan asserts, 'because it's something they would never have had the chance to do otherwise. A lot of people at that age want to prove to themselves that they can do something, and they want to prove to their parents that they can do something and do it well. You've heard of the RSC, you know of it. I think the idea of performing there makes you feel worthy.' Ryan's assessment here touches on the neo-liberal, and the difficult relationship the idea of aspiration holds within issues of class discourse. If engagement with the RSC is positioned as an ideal, we risk our programmes becoming systems of class shifting, where working-class participants are shaped and moulded into a more middle-class ideal. Although this may be seen to offer individual benefit to participants, it does little to address or articulate the societal and political systems responsible for the inequality in the first place. Juliet Rufford argues that it is 'not the job' of theatres to 'fulfil the proper function of the state,'[35] and Ryan's statement here gets to the moral dilemma at the heart of theatre engagement more broadly. Within the context of Shakespeare, where we could argue that the traditional role models of organisations such as the Royal Shakespeare Company are the embodiment of middle-class ideals, whether we can engage working-class participants on their own terms, and how aspiration both encourages and complicates that, is something we must be atuned to as facilitators.

A repeated finding in our own, and others, work, is that students expressed an increased engagement with Shakespeare when it provided a clear link to their own biography, background or status. 'Learning,' says Peter Jarvis, 'is the transformation of our experiences.'[36] In our discussion, Ryan alluded to the concept of the 'safe space,' an environment in which the sharing of our own biographical experience is both encouraged and protected, as an entry point to allow us to engage with new material through this personal lens. For Nick Bagnall, the failure of a system to provide a connection between the reality of his own lived experience as a working-class student in Scarborough and the necessity of learning Shakespeare's work without question, was a step in the wrong direction. This isn't to dictate an overemphasis on 'relevance' but to allow students the chance for an honest debate to the question, 'what's the point?' Education outside of the classroom can allow such questions to seem less taboo; students engagement is experiential, not simply because of the use of active pedagogy, but from the specific association and conditioning of a non-classroom space that facilitates risk taking and personal enquiry. This is not to imply that schools do not use active pedagogy – drama, music and art are just some examples of subjects where the learning experience can differ substantially from what we might deem as standard. In this case, we must look to how the space itself signals its desire for play and creativity. With the exception of schools with additional resources, many 'drama studios' are empty classrooms with the addition of some lights and blackout curtains, at best. But the signaling of the space as a studio, the play and behavior encouraged and teased through hidden space, darkness and light, and the freedom from sitting behind desks, renegotiate a learning environment in which students are invited to learn differently. Ryan recalls her own English Literature lessons, in which her teacher would take the class into the school field to act out parts of *Wuthering Heights* and *Macbeth*. The novelty factor could be at play here, but for those students who find traditional schooling restrictive, including those from a lower socio-economic background where relationships with education may have been worn down over generations, in which classrooms and teachers become associated with authority and rules, thinking about how the learning environment signals cooperation and engagement may provide further steps towards connecting students with the potential of storytelling.

Participants in amateur theatre uncover the 'point' of a production together through shared enquiry, in an environment where, 'both cast and spectators are at play together.'[37] Pleasure and learning, as observed by Claire Cochrane, does not have to be devalued by an activity's so-called amateur status, but can affect the transformation of an experience into, 'part of their own personal, local, bodily memories.'[38] If the purpose of presenting ownership back to the learner is to engender a range of responses and voices, we need to explore how to encourage those voices in ways that are valid to them. In short, we have to promote the risk of failure. In doing so, we move into an environment in which every voice belongs.

Why Shakespeare?

"If Shakespeare had never existed', he asked, 'would the world have differed much from what it is to-day?'"[39] Through Mr Ramsay, Virginia Woolf poses a question we can be accused of overlooking in Britain, in a system where, all too often, Shakespeare is seen as, 'sustaining the identity of Western civilization.'[40] Michael D. Bristol expands, stating that 'Shakespeare's importance is illusory; people can get along perfectly well without him.'[41] It is a question that facilitators and teachers must allow to resurface, to see beyond Shakespeare as either a cultural or curriculum necessity, to allow learners to develop a relationship with the work that is defined on their own terms. This is of particular relevance when working with those from a background or community 'for whom theatricality is not intrinsic.'[42] We must not assume that Shakespeare is important to our students' lives, but allow them to reach their own conclusions about this, for themselves.

When asked why, or if, Shakespeare is important, Ryan replied that 'with Shakespeare.... you get the whole spectrum of people; you get a king and a servant and everything in between. You hear everyone's story; every voice is involved... you can see yourself represented.' This summary requires us to be imaginative in our approach to casting and participation, to think beyond binaries of gender, ethnicity and status, to allow students to engage with the raw text without cultural inheritance or societal norms. 'It is not Shakespeare's place on the curriculum that is detrimental', writes Purewal, 'rather it is outdated pedagogical practices.'[43] But the adaptability of Shakespeare's material, in his characters, performance opportunities and in the vast wealth of interpretation throughout our projects, media and lives, is what gives practitioners their greatest asset in promoting engagement. Writing of the work of applied theatre practitioners, Monica Prendergast and Juliana Saxton characterise issue-based, socially focused theatre as being performed 'by actors who are intentionally hidden behind the mask of character.'[44] The concept of the mask is an important one. The emotional extremity of Shakespeare's prose, the language itself, when tackled with confidence, may actually provide a distance through which performers can engage with emotions and scenarios that are both distant from and familiar to their own. This can be of benefit to anybody engaging with Shakespeare in performance, but for participants from a working-class background, the text provides an opportunity through which we can empower participants to understand aspects of their own lives. Thus, rather than providing aspiration towards a middle-class ideal, we are able to support students to understand their own lives and have agency over the forces that shape it. This catharsis of experience can be transformative for student confidence, demonstrated by the wealth of continued engagement of the alumni of PurpleCoat.

Michael Etherton writes that 'impact may manifest itself in many forms.'[45] We cannot satisfactorily measure the effect of non-formal experiences of Shakespeare through quantitative measures. We are not seeking for short-term effect that is simply 'an immediate assessment of achievement'; rather we aim to understand the specific requirements of our own community in order to continue to serve that community's needs.[46] Short-term financial or political motives may create projects where, 'change may not coincide with the desires of the community.'[47] By being part of the community, and by identifying ourselves as equal members of it, we can begin to build trust where prior inhibitions may attempt to be recalculated. Each workshop at Meladrama began with a statement of my background, an equalising of risk and of opportunity. In this aspect, the concept of the safe space must first be risked by the facilitator, in order to show participants that failure is acceptable and encouraged as a necessary step towards development. This is particularly important against a working-class background, where failure may be tied with different associations of survival and belonging. In the intersection between active pedagogy, risk and student experience lies the basis for an engagement with classical theatre that is experienced on one's own terms. In taking this risk, we cannot attempt to predict or shape a student's acquisition of Shakespeare's work. Where this may be familiar to facilitators, for educators it may be a step into the unknown, in an environment where 'restrictive' curriculum places focus instead on 'technique-spotting' and an 'obsession with vocabulary.'[48] Even with these considerations in place, we are still challenged to discover whether a participant's engagement, enjoyment and achievement derives from the process or the material. When considering the workshop participants and alumni who chose not to respond to my calls for feedback, we are challenged to avoid formulating feedback that excludes these silent voices. Perhaps the voices that can complete the picture are those who chose not to respond at all.

Binary divisions between class, or between the amateur and professional, are those that create groups that form the 'intersubjective recognition' of our identity.[49] PurpleCoat's social aims and funding situation prevented a description of the company's work as being 'professional'. Yet the alternative, 'amateur', suggested values that belied the high standards to which the work aspired. These definitions suggest a concrete dualism that reduces theatrical participation to an either/or scenario. We simply need to move beyond systems and solutions that operate on a two-pronged basis, marginalising the wealth of contexts into two ideologically opposing camps. We need, 'a more inclusive attention towards community values,' in order to best understand how to develop them.[50] Occupying the midground between paid and participatory work, and in its overt aim to, 'reassert or undermine socio-political norms', this chapter has provided a focus of PurpleCoat and Meladrama's socio-economic context within which their work is produced.[51] This work inhabits a realm of inherent contradiction, not least in the role of the facilitator, who may, 'come to represent a threat to cultural diversity as agents of development's monoculture.'[52] If we are to find positive ways of encouraging previously excluded communities to express a relationship with Shakespeare, we need to work hard to address our role models and our motivations. James Farrell, of the RSC Open Stages, observed that 'teaching a room full of seasoned theatre practitioners who are not subject to the kinds of industry demands that drama students are, means that participants are much more likely to ask difficult questions',[53] and we must embrace this provocation as an opportunity to successfully address questions of relevance and connection. Only when we do so, can we encourage participants to see Shakespeare as having significance beyond the need to pass formal exams. Only when we do so, can we enable our communities to take ownership of Shakespeare for themselves.

Acknowledgements

I am indebted to Rowan MacKenzie and Robert Shaughnessy for their comments and suggestions in process of writing this chapter. Thanks also to Michael Dobson, Kelly Hunter and Abigail Rokison-Woodall, whose feedback and questioning helped to formulate and focus of my research. Special thanks to Tracy Irish whose support and guidance as a supervisor was indispensable.

Karl Falconer is a theatre director from Liverpool, England, whose work has been screened and staged across the UK and Ireland. His is currently working with the Paul Hamlyn Foundation on Purple-Door, the UK's first free theatre, and with the Shakespeare North Playhouse, as well as completing his doctorate at Royal Holloway. He has developed publications with Routledge helping theatre-makers to start their own companies. He is part of the Northern Broadsides Advisory Squad, helping to develop sustainability in their practice.

Notes

1. Vanessa Thorpe, 'Why does British Theatre Leave Working-Class Actors in the Wings?', *Guardian*, 8 July 2018.
2. Michael Dobson, *Shakespeare and Amateur Performance* (Cambridge: Cambridge University Press, 2011), 1.
3. Graeme Paton, 'National Curriculum Overhaul: Pupils to Study More Shakespeare', *Daily Telegraph*, 8 July 2013; Emma Perry and Becky Francis, *The Social Class Gap for Educational Achievement: a review of the literature*, (RSA Projects, Research Report, 1 December 2010): 2.
4. David Gruenewald, 'The Best of Both Worlds: A Critical Pedagogy of Place', *Educational Researcher*, 32, no.4 (2003): 5.
5. *Shakespeare Schools Festival* (2019) Available at https://www.shakespeareschools.org/ (accessed 11 March 2019); *PurpleCoat Productions* (2019) Available at http://www.purplecoatproductions.com/ (accessed 11 March 2019).
6. Neville Ellis and Tony Loughland, 'The Challenges of Practitioner Research: A Comparative Study of Singapore and NSW', *Australian Journal of Teacher Education*, 41, no.2 (2016): 122; Michael Etherton and Tim Prentki, 'Drama for Change? Prove It! Impact Assessment in Applied Theatre', *Research in Drama Education*, 11, no.2 (2006): 141.
7. 'Further decline in Arts Education 2020–2021,' *Theatre Workout*, 18 October 2021 https://www.theatreworkout.com/post/further-decline-in-arts-education-2020-2021 (accessed 14 September 2022).
8. Georgia Snow, 'National Theatre's cheap tickets in doubt as Travelex pulls sponsorship after 15 years', *The Stage*, 3 Oct 2018; *Royal National Theatre* (2019) Available at www.nationaltheatre.org.uk (accessed 11 March 2019).
9. *Royal Shakespeare Company* (2019) Available at https://www.rsc.org.uk/ (accessed 11 March 2019); Brian Lighthill, 'Shakespeare– an endangered species?' *English in Education*, 45 (2011): 37.
10. Jessica Gelt, '"We're driving straight up the cliff.' Theatre is back, but recovery proves perilous,' *LA Times*, 11 May 2022. Available at https://www.latimes.com/entertainment-arts/story/2022-05-11/theater-is-back-attendance-is-down-costs-soaring-covid-19-pandemic (accessed 14 September 2022).
11. Dobson, *Shakespeare and Amateur Performance*, 198.
12. Lyn Gardner, 'Arts Council releases report on state of English theatre', *Guardian*, 20 October 2016.
13. *Donmar Warehouse* (2019) Available at https://www.donmarwarehouse.com/ (accessed 11 March 2019); *Young Vic* (2019) Available at https://www.youngvic.org/ (accessed 11 March 2019); *Liverpool Everyman and Playhouse Theatres* (2019) Available at https://www.everymanplayhouse.com/ (accessed 11 March 2019); *All-Female Trilogy*, dir. by Phyllida Lloyd (London: Donmar Warehouse, 2012–2016); *Twelfth Night*, dir. by Kwame Kwei-Armah and Oskar Eustis (New York, The Public Theatre and London, The Young Vic 2018); *Othello*, dir. by Gemma Bodinetz (Liverpool, 2018).
14. Sandeep Purewal, 'Shakespeare in the classroom: to be or not to be?', *Warwick Journal of Education – Transforming Teaching*, 1 (2017) 27.
15. Andrew Murphy, *Shakespeare for the People: Working-Class Readers 1800–1900* (Cambridge: Cambridge University Press, 2008).

16. 'The Shakespearian Commemoration – Its Blunders and Its Failures,' *Reynold's Newspapers*, 1 May 1864.
17. Murphy, *Shakespeare for the People*, 3.
18. Ibid.
19. 'Profile: John Prescott', *BBC News*, 27 August 2007, http://news.bbc.co.uk/1/hi/uk_politics/6636565.stm (accessed 10 July 2018).
20. 'The Great British Class Calculator: What Class Are You?', *BBC News*, 3 Apr 2013, https://www.bbc.co.uk/news/magazine-22000973?economic-income=0.175&economic-propertytype=rent&economic-property=0&economic-property=0.16&economic-savings=0 (accessed 1 June 2018).
21. Sharon O'Dair, *Class, Critics and Shakespeare: Bottom Lines on the Culture Wars* (Ann Arbor: Michigan University Press, 2000), 2.
22. Ian Hall, 'An Interview with Nick Bagnall', *Liverpool Sound and Vision*, 28 October 2016.
23. Geoff Petty, *Teaching Today: A Practical Guide*, 4th Edition (Cheltenham: Nelson Thornes Ltd, 2009).
24. Sian Adiseshiah, '"Chavs' 'Gyppos' and 'Scum'? Class in Twenty-First Century Drama', in *Twenty-First Century Drama: What Happens Now?*, ed. Sian Adiseshiah and Louise LePage (London: Palgrave Macmillan, 2016), 154.
25. Melanie Ash, 'Home Page', Meladrama (2018) http://meladrama.co.uk/ (accessed 1 May 2018).
26. Joe Winston and Miles Tandy, *Beginning Shakespeare: 4–11: Active Approaches for Early Encounters* (London: Routledge, 2012). See also Cicely Berry, *From Word to Play: A Handbook for Directors* (London: Oberon, 2008); Barbara Houseman, *Tackling Text and Subtext: A Step-by-Step Guide for Actors* (London: Nick Hern Books, 2008); John Barton, *Playing Shakespeare* (London: Bloomsbury, 2009).
27. John Dewey, 'My Pedagogic Creed', *School Journal*, 54 (1897), 78.
28. Natasha Ryan, interview by Karl Falconer, (London, 6 June 2018). All subsequent quotations are taken from this interview.
29. Gaby Hinsliff, 'Why the Working Class Loose Out on the Career Ladder', *Guardian*, 26 January 2017; Holly-Rae Smith and Milan Rai, 'Hard-won working-class confidence', *Peace News*, January 2018, https://peacenews.info/node/8943/hard-won-working-class-confidence (accessed 1 August 2018).
30. Patsy Rodenburg, *The Right to Speak: Working with the Voice*, 2nd edition (London: Bloomsbury, 2015), 12.
31. Jessica McCrory Calarco, '"I Need Help!' Social Class and Children's Help Seeking in Elementary School', *American Sociological Review*, 76, no.6 (2011), 862.
32. Vik Loveday, 'Working-Class Participation: Middle-Class Aspiration? Value, Upward Mobility and Symbolic Indebtedness in Higher Education', *The Sociological Review*, 63, no.1 (2015), 578.
33. Donna Ferguson, 'Working-class children get less of everything in education, including respect', *Guardian*, 21 November 2017.
34. Nicholas Burbles and Rupert Beck, 'Critical Thinking and Critical Pedagogy: Relations, Differences and Limits', in *Critical Theories in Education: Changing Terrains of Knowledge and Politics*, ed. Thomas Popkewitz and Lynn Fendler (New York: Routledge, 1999), 50.
35. Juliet Rufford, *Theatre and Architecture* (London: Palgrave Macmillan, 2015).

36. Peter Jarvis, *Adult Education and Lifelong Learning: Theory and Practice*, 4th edition (London: Routledge, 2010), 37.
37. Dobson, *Shakespeare and Amateur Performance*, 203.
38. Claire Cochrane, 'The Pervasiveness of the Commonplace: The Historian and Amateur Theatre', *Theatre Research International*, 26, no.3 (2001), 233; Dobson, *Shakespeare and Amateur Performance,* 216.
39. Virginia Woolf, *To the Lighthouse* (Oxford: Oxford University Press, 2006), 30.
40. Michael Bristol, *Big-Time Shakespeare* (London: Routledge, 1996), 12.
41. Ibid., 6.
42. Monica Prendergast and Juliana Saxton (eds), *Applied Theatre: International Case Studies and Challenges for Practice* (Bristol: Intellect, 2009), 12.
43. Purewal, 'Shakespeare in the Classroom,' 32.
44. Prendergast and Saxton, *Applied Theatre*,12.
45. Etherton and Prentki, 'Drama for Change?', 140.
46. Ibid.
47. Ibid., 141.
48. Catherine Lough, 'English teachers criticise 'restrictive' curriculum,' *TES,* 18 July 2019 https://www.tes.com/magazine/archive/english-teachers-criticise-restrictive-curriculum (accessed 14 September 2022).
49. Axel Honneth, *The Struggle for Recognition: The Moral Grammar of Social Conflicts* (Cambridge, MA: MIT Press, 1995), 5.
50. Cochrane, 'The Pervasiveness of the Commonplace', 236.
51. Prendergast and Saxton, *Applied Theatre*, 8.
52. Etherton and Prentki, 'Drama for Change?', 141.
53. Helen Nicholson, Nadine Holdsworth and Molly Flynn, *For love or money? Collaborations between amateur and professional theatre in the Royal Shakespeare Company's Open Stages Programme. Project Report.* AHRC, University of Warwick, Royal Holloway University of London, 2016, p.15.

Chapter 5
'Branches of Learning'
Collaborative Cognitive and Affective Learning Between Shakespearean Students trained in Schools, Universities and Carceral Institutions

Shelia T. Cavanagh and Steve Rowland

London's Wandsworth Prison, one of the largest prisons in the United Kingdom, has housed numerous renowned inmates, including Oscar Wilde, James Earl Ray, the Kray Twins, and Ronnie Biggs, one of the 'Great Train Robbers.' Its diligent, but unofficial, historian and archivist, Stewart McLaughlin, details some of the rules governing this institution's inhabitants during the nineteenth century, when prisoners were housed and fed in single cells, talking was forbidden and 'Male prisoners were required to wear a mask whenever leaving the cell and in the company of other prisoners. Female prisoners wore a dark veil.'[1] The prohibitions against speaking and showing one's face demonstrates the guiding ethos governing the prison environment in this period; namely, that social

Notes for this section begin on page 83.

interaction between prisoners, whether visual or auditory, threatens institutional peace and stability. Isolation, silence, and an inability to recognize one another, on the other hand, could foster an environment conducive for calm and order.

Wandsworth's nineteenth century rules against communication between prison inhabitants defies the principles underlying contemporary 'Shakespeare in Prison' programmes, including those discussed in this chapter. Whether based on performance or discussion, these current endeavors generally emphasize the role of respectful interaction between people in their efforts to use Shakespearean drama effectively in a prison environment. Just as high school and university Shakespearean classrooms tend to rely upon personal and intellectual interaction between students to increase their facility with the written and performed text, educators in prison often place a premium on improved interpersonal skills as a central goal of their pedagogical enterprise, even when the prisoners are largely kept apart, as Laura Bates describes in 2013's *Shakespeare Saved My Life*, which focuses on studying Shakespeare in solitary confinement.[2] Sadly, recent assessments of Wandsworth's accomplishments in the 21st century suggest that efforts there may still not meet such standards.[3] The international proliferation of strong educational programmes in prisons, including those with emphases on Shakespeare, however, suggests that Wandsworth and other facilities have numerous models they can emulate, if they choose to improve conditions for inmates. Here, we will focus on hybrid models of prison instruction whereby current and formerly incarcerated students study in concert with more traditional college and high school students.[4]

Monroe Correctional Facility and Emory University

This chapter describes some of the ways that prison programmes can operate effectively, but it also details significant differences between standard undergraduate and high school classes and their counterparts for incarcerated Shakespeare students. The authors share an active goal of reducing the gap they experience between these two kinds of classroom experiences, but continue to consider this a challenge in the Shakespeare courses they link. In fact, we suggest that an approach to teaching Shakespeare which encourages students to understand themselves and respectfully talk and listen may be a model which would work well in both traditional and prison classrooms. Here, we will describe two partnerships: one with some students studying at Emory University in Atlanta, in concert with others participating at Monroe Correctional Facility in Washington State and the second with Formerly Incarcerated Teachers [FITs] from Woodbourne Correctional Facility in New York and students at the University of Georgia and educational institutions across the United States through a new educational nonprofit entitled Time Out of Joint [TOOJ]. The Emory/Monroe partnership was established, despite the participants' geographical divide, partially because the prisons proximate to Emory have now been moved a significant distance away, but also because Sheila T. Cavanagh, Founding Director of the World Shakespeare Project, has a long-standing commitment to establishing innovative collaborations in order to facilitate advanced Shakespearean involvement with populations facing significant access challenges. The instructors would prefer to have the students address each other directly through videoconferencing, but prison officials currently forbid this.[5] As an alternative, students are placed into groups with members of each cohort, who exchange and respond to each other's written assignments. Cavanagh teaches the Emory class in person and makes occasional visits to the Monroe sessions. Steve Rowland, an award-winning documentary producer and educator, takes the lead at Monroe, but regularly participates in Atlanta classes through videoconferencing. Some prison programmes bring university undergraduate students directly into prison classrooms. Distance makes that impossible for the Monroe/Emory collaboration, but the instructors endeavor to create a shared enterprise that brings each group of students into significant communication with each other.[6]

Rowland and Cavanagh work together effectively, but continue to contend with disjunctures related to the learning aspects of these courses, since the aims include both intellectually rigorous study of Shakespeare and the kinds of achievements commonly associated with what Benjamin Bloom and others term 'affective' learning.[7] Bloom's taxonomy has received considerable scholarly attention since it first appeared, but the situation he describes often still holds true: 'Although there are affective consequences of all teaching-learning activities, and although representative statements of objectives of local curricula often contain hopes for affective as well as cognitive outcomes, the typical school examines for cognitive changes only.'⁸ Such challenges may appear in any such joint pedagogical undertaking, but they emerge here particularly prominently because the Monroe students receive written feedback but no course credit or grades for their work, while the Emory undergraduates are graded for their contributions to the course and enroll in order to complete college degree requirements. The differences between these students, therefore, extend beyond their distinctive 'local habitation[s],' (A *Midsummer Night's Dream* 5.1) and regularly influence both the kinds of challenges they undertake and their responses to the conversations this brand of Shakespearean collaboration generates. Students in conventional college classrooms are often reticent about the personal exposure frequently associated with affective learning, while some (by no means all) of the Monroe students feel intimidated by the academic prowess of their Emory counterparts, who tend to have more formal and conventional cognitive training.

The well-known Shakespeare Behind Bars Programme (SBB), founded and directed by Curt L. Tofteland, illustrates some of the 'affective' tenets that make SBB so successful, but simultaneously impede easy transfer to a more conventional undergraduate setting. Cavanagh was fortunate to spend several days in 2017 with Tofteland and SBB at Michigan's Earnest C. Brooks and West Shoreline Correctional Facilities. She also participated in a workshop on 'creating circles of trust' that Tofteland led at the 2017 'Arts in Corrections: Building Bridges to the Future' Conference sponsored by California Lawyers for the Arts, the William James Association, and Loyola Marymount University. Tofteland has also visited Emory classrooms in person and through videoconferencing, and we have been honored to welcome SBB alumnus Sammie Byron to classes at Emory after he was released from the Luther Luckett Correctional Complex. Each of these experiences has confirmed what the SBB documentary demonstrates; namely, that SBB 'circles of trust' (now called 'circles of truth') initiate and support powerful sites for transformative work.⁹

As Tofteland's course materials indicate, 'a Shakespeare Behind Bars Restorative Circle of Reconciliation is built on the most prized core values that each member of the circle-of-trust has pledged to honor.'¹⁰ The qualities thus introduced typically include such things as 'honesty,' 'empathy,' 'fairness,' 'confidentiality,' 'courage,' and 'forgiveness.'¹¹ Once these operating principles are in place, those participating are encouraged to trust in 'the safety of our circle'¹² as they face and express intersections between their work on Shakespeare (and other topics) and their own lives. Often, these sessions require significant emotional risk-taking; the circles, therefore, are created to nurture those participating in a protective environment where they may choose to challenge themselves intellectually, physically, spiritually, and/or emotionally.

Rowland's work at Monroe does not focus on Shakespearean performance, but focuses on critical analysis and discussions of the plays, as well as reading out loud. Inspired by Tofteland, Rowland too begins each prison class session with a circle of trust. While not affiliated with SBB, his pedagogical vision also encourages self-reflection and personal growth as an explicit part of the educational enterprise. The results are frequently life-changing for Monroe students and for Atlanta undergraduates. Emory students report gratitude at being involved in these discussions engaged in through shared writing, and are often delighted at the fresh insights the prisoners, drawing on their life experiences bring to the plays. The Shakespearean prisoners who choose education set a very interesting model for the undergraduates. It is eye-opening to meet incarcerated people who are committed to learning in deep ways for their own intellectual and spiritual growth.

The conversations generated within and between the classrooms in Atlanta and Monroe are typically powerful and insightful, but the instructors need to take special care to generate a parallel environment between the two constituencies. Students who are being graded understandably worry that taking risks could jeopardize their chance at academic success. Producing a rubric that builds and supports the level of trust needed for them to participate productively is possible, but not straightforward. In addition, encouraging undergraduates to draw parallels between their own experiences and what they find in Shakespeare can stall on stories of 'love at first sight,' in contrast to the incarcerated students who more readily recognize their lives in the violent urges of Hotspur and Macbeth as well as in the complicated power dynamics presented in the plays. While students in both pedagogical environments often demonstrate considerable intellectual prowess, fundamental differences between their educational backgrounds, life histories, and academic goals provide significant, but productive tensions when their Shakespearean realms are brought together in this way. Cavanagh's faculty position at Emory requires her to keep assessment and scholarly achievement clearly in place, while Rowland's role as the instructor of a non-credit-bearing course enables him to encourage more personal introspection and reflection. Both pedagogical perspectives can be rigorous and productive. Bringing them together creates challenges, but these obstacles seem well-worth the effort involved. As part of this work, we take the energy and insight currently fueling international Shakespearean scholarship and performance into both classrooms in order to help each group feel connected to life outside their immediate environment. This strategy explores ways this sort of collaboration enhances the learning of both groups. The prisoners frequently see themselves inside the characters, or imagine how they would confront the crises depicted in the play. Prisoners are quick to recognize and comprehend the emotional resonances of *Macbeth, Hamlet, King Lear, The Merchant of Venice, Othello, Julius Caesar, Coriolanus, Measure for Measure, The Tempest* and so many others. These understandings often help them define new, productive life paths for themselves, an outcome that strengthens the idea that 'Shakespeare Changes Lives,' and supports our commitment to expanding Shakespearean study to a variety of non-conventional settings. There are many reasons that students in prison want to study Shakespeare: past familiarity with the plays; long-time curiosity; an interest in writing or acting; or perhaps a desire to insist that 'Shakespeare belongs to everyone.' Too many of these men have grown up as total outsiders to society, believing deeply that access to even a modest, healthy life is not available to them. While reading the works of many writers can be powerful, giving inmates who feel like outsiders access to Shakespeare and encouraging them to discuss it with students studying in more traditional settings facilitates empowering conversations for all concerned.

Rowland was introduced to teaching Shakespeare inside prisons in 2010 by Arin Arbus, a talented Shakespearean director at Theater for A New Audience in NYC, who invited him to document one of her classes (under the auspices of Katherine Vockins and Rehabilitation Through the Arts or RTA) through film at Woodbourne Correctional Facility in upstate New York. Arbus is adept at working with actors, but she is also an expert at getting to the emotional meat of the plays. Her ability to lead a class reading *Macbeth* engage in open discussion is remarkable. Rowland was impressed by what he saw and learned that day. The men in the class included former drug dealers, gang members, armed robbers, and even some who said they were innocent or political prisoners. They united despite their differences to create an environment of careful listening, humor and mutual respect and demonstrated a joy in learning. Those who participated exhibited great intelligence, critical and analytical thinking. They also spoke with striking command and articulation of their ideas. Further, there was a sense of kindness, humor and camaraderie in the room. This remarkable afternoon changed Rowland's life. Arbus's approach and the students' responses made it clear that this model of teaching and talking about the plays could be deeply transformative, in part because it helps connect two aspects of our brains and beings – here described as the cognitive and affective. Rowland realizes that bringing together these two avenues has been at the core of his decades of work using the arts as a way to open people's minds and awaken their souls. The arts open us up – both intellectually and emotionally – and studying great art – whether Cervantes, or Coltrane or Shakespeare or August Wilson – forces us to think critically and understand the world on multiple levels. We need to be aware of society and social issues, history, psychology, writing styles, story-telling, the history of literature, gender issues, and so much more.

A few years later Rowland served as the head interviewer at the Globe-to-Globe festival in London, and subsequently was able to create a Global Shakespeare workshop based on three G2G videos offered by Shakespeare's Globe. The 5-day workshop, called 'Shakespeare and Me', co-facilitated by Josie Whittlesey (who would later found The Drama Club, NYC), was filmed and is the basis for Rowland's upcoming film *Time Out of Joint: Prison Reflections on Shakespeare*, and for TOOJ, a new series of educational workshops co-led by the now former educated prisoners.

One of the first choices made in teaching Shakespeare is whether to concentrate on performance or reading. Some instructors consider the plays from a directorial perspective, coaching actors to perform. Others focus more prominently on reading these dramatic texts, an approach that demands choices about ways to bring the stories to life and make them understandable, relevant and powerful for different populations. In addition, there are strategies for reading the plays that can loosely be identified as academic or experiential. Cavanagh and Rowland aim to combine these approaches to make this engagement meaningful and useful to prisoners and undergraduates. The academic – more cognitive – approach, teaches analysis, organized thinking, strong writing, and uses the plays as lenses to think about wide-ranging issues. The 'affective' route reads the plays as an actor might. Why is the character saying these particular words at this point? What is he/she trying to accomplish? Putting an emphasis on the people involved begins to give us an understanding of major issues of power, love, betrayal, lust, secrecy, lying, gender switching and more. On the whole, prisoners tend to be particularly astute at this kind of character analysis and understanding. Cavanagh and Rowland work to integrate these two approaches, finding ways to teach across many different levels of experience and literacy. Shakespeare facilitates valuable discussions that incorporate both cognitive and affective learning, however. There are a number of challenges to teaching Shakespeare at a place like Monroe that are made more complex by integrating the classes with undergraduate students at Emory. There is a wide range of prior experience among prison students in reading, writing and with Shakespeare. The commitment in the 'Shakespeare and Me' course has been to accept all students and make all interested people welcome. Some students are absolute novices. Others are deeply invested in Shakespeare and have read many of the plays, and in a few instances, have read all of them. There are also some issues about diversity in the classes. Prison populations are complex and relationships between prisoners can be strained. The stereotype of prison hierarchy often holds true, with serious prejudices, for example, against inmates convicted of sex crimes.

Despite these complications, connecting the classes at Monroe and Emory has been accomplished with relative ease, although we were only able to exchange essays between the two locations. This process has been a delight for students in both worlds. The Emory students are deeply appreciative of getting connected to the prisoners. Like many Americans, they typically believe initially that prisoners are incapable of having intelligent ideas, be able to read a Shakespeare play, or even to have feelings. The prisoners love the idea of a student – to- student exchange of ideas and exploration. They get a boost by having people in the outside world know that they exist. We inevitably hit snags in this process, however. The first time we introduced the exchange, we asked students on each side to write about past experiences with Shakespeare, including what they liked, didn't like, were afraid of, etc. They were also asked to talk about why they were taking the class, and what they hoped to gain.

This exchange went beautifully. The following semester, however, the Atlanta class convened several weeks before Monroe started. We began, therefore, with Emory student papers about *Merchant of Venice*. Some of the prisoners were nearly stopped in their tracks by this experience of a collegiate writing style. They assumed that this was the kind of writing that was always expected and desired in the real world. While the Emory papers were strong, however, there was a detachment in the Emory students' writing that focused solely on cognitive learning rather than the affective perspective honed in 'Shakespeare and Me.' This initial glitch got the semester off to an awkward start, but the students eventually became willing and able to communicate effectively with each other.

One of the prison students, displayed his considerable critical skills, writing a paper in which he compared the sins of *Macbeth* to some of his own, wrote the following:

> It is the small faint voice, indistinct and tremulous, that whispers through our minds like a gentle but persistent wind in recognition of our mis-steps, or, the strident claxon that storms rhythmically through your being in triumph over the dark desolation of your sleepless nights in recognition of sins committed, and it is that which carries the onus of our choices, that cringes at our shallow cruelties, but yet elates at the selfless antics of a puppy. (Monroe/Emory exchange)

His ability to tie his own crime to those of the characters in the play allowed us all to see the power in what we were attempting to do.

As this example suggests, we believe that it is important to ask all students to open up and see their own true nature, including aspects of themselves that are kind, intelligent and loving (or angry) at the same time that they learn analytical skills. This process is particularly, but not exclusively, significant for incarcerated students. A majority of prisoners in US correctional facilities have lived hellish lives. They are too often victims of abuse. They frequently see themselves as having no chance to succeed in the 'game' of education that is restricted, in their minds, to the middle- and upper-class white world. Now, in prison, they are surrounded by guards who bully them, and have to find ways to navigate the imminent dangers that are always present 'inside'. In addition, far too many of the prisoners have little in the way of outside role models – people who can model any sort of normal behavior that will serve them well as they learn and upon leaving prison. In typical undergraduate classes, cognitive skills predominate, which can leave the students disconnected from the relationship between their humanity and the intellectual material they cover. This course endeavors to integrate these different goals for all students involved, in order to make all their experiences richer.

In response, our assignments endeavor to tap into both cognitive and affective skills and outcomes for the students. Each group of students write essays following standard rules for formatting and citation, and include substantial passages from the plays, but they simultaneously correlate Shakespeare to their own experiences and reflect on both the texts and the life choices each writer presents in their contributions. These exchanges are often profound, bringing new perspectives to bear for students in each setting. When discussing *Henry IV: Part One*, for example, typical American university students often report struggling with their parents' expectations as Hal apparently does, but they typically see Falstaff as a comic, fairly benign figure. Our incarcerated students respond thoughtfully, empathetically and sometimes challengingly to the personal stories included by the Emory students, but they commonly view Falstaff as a more dangerous and disruptive figure than the undergraduates see. Many of the Monroe writers describe figures they label as 'Falstaffs,' who helped lead the incarcerated men astray and contributed to the paths leading to prison. One man emotionally recounted the recent demise of his own 'Falstaff,' proclaiming that he hoped authorities had 'welded the urn holding his ashes shut' so that no one would ever encounter his malevolent influence again. Such exchanges regularly speak powerfully in personal ways to all involved, while deepening their engagement and understanding of Shakespeare's texts.

These Shakespeare classes, therefore, allow students to explore facets of humanity accessible through this drama as well as its literary devices. There are limits to this approach, of course. The classroom should not become a therapy room, but therapeutic things can happen. This tricky balance requires experienced teachers who take small steps and reflect carefully in order to find an appropriate path with each group of students. It is that opening of the heart, that link to humanity, that is really going to help each student achieve future success. Our Emory students invariably announce that they are going to treasure their copies of the Monroe exchanges throughout their lives. New undergraduates enroll because they have heard about the remarkable experiences this process generates. In addition to his work at Monroe, Rowland is in touch with well over 20 graduates of the RTA programme he filmed in NYC.[13] Many of the students he worked with there have established successful lives outside of prison, finding ways to temper youthful rage and become functioning citizens, employees and in many cases, husbands and fathers. The sense of connection created in these classrooms can have lasting repercussions, as one of Rowland's students in NY's Woodbourne prison discovered. 'Casper' was part of the 2010 RTA programme where Rowland began filming interviews as part of the film *Time Out of Joint: Prison Reflections on Shakespeare* he now uses regularly in TOOJ collaborations (www.TOOJ.org). Several video clips were posted to Rowland's website without fanfare. There was no indication that anyone even knew about them. Surprisingly, therefore, in 2013, when Rowland returned to Woodbourne, he was greeted with a beaming smile from Casper, who offered sincere thanks. 'For what?' Rowland asked. He said, 'That video of me talking about *Romeo and Juliet* helped me get parole!' 'How so?' Rowland wondered. Casper explained that at Woodbourne, men almost never receive parole on their first hearing – instead they are asked to return every 2 years until the parole board shows them some mercy. Casper had just gone to his first hearing. He said that despite a stack of certificates showing he had taken nearly every class imaginable in the prison and received his BA from Bard while incarcerated, the review was not going well. The parole board members did not think he had proven that he was really a reformed man. His heart sank at the thought of waiting at least two more years in prison. Then one of the reviewers said – 'I know you – I have seen you somewhere before...... oh, I know, I saw you in that video. Tell me the truth, did you really read Shakespeare?' 'Yes, Ma'am,' he replied. I did. I love Shakespeare' – She tested him on the spot – *Romeo & Juliet, Merchant of Venice, Macbeth, Hamlet, Twelfth Night* – he knew them all. She was delighted and they had a long chat about Shakespeare and how prisoners can be enlightened by reading and talking about the plays. His ability to talk about feminism, manhood and power convinced her that he had, in fact, reformed. Casper was given parole after that first hearing and has been out of prison for over seven years. He works as a counselor to young men in NYC. Recently married, he now has a young daughter and continues to be remorseful for his choices as a teenager.

Time Out of Joint

As noted, several of the Woodbourne Shakespeare alumni are now being paid as teachers in TOOJ, a videoconferencing project bringing together high school and university students, using conversations, performance exercises, and texts from Shakespeare and participants in order to introduce young students to the varied cognitive and affective benefits of learning about life and Shakespeare from a group of (Formerly Incarcerated Teachers) FITs who offer considerable intellectual and life learning developed through their complex histories. The initiative also includes segments from Rowland's film, which also includes excerpts from the 2012 Globe-to-Globe project at Shakespeare's Globe in London. Currently, Rowland helps coordinate workshops including TOOJ participants Amiti Bey, Tariq Beaudouin, Mohendra Singh, and Kwame McLean in conjunction with both college and high school students. Cavanagh serves on the advisory board. The project has received a Teaching with Primary Sources grant from the Library of Congress[14] and a grant from Humanities New York (HNY) through their new programme called 'Post-Incarceration Humanities Partnerships.' The 2022 collaborations have been profound and successful, with many of the student participants requesting additional sessions.

In some TOOJ sessions, students and FITs explore issues arising in Shakespearean drama and in the participants' own experiences, such as the imbalance of power demonstrated by Angelo's efforts in *Measure for Measure* to coerce the young nun Isabella into having sex with him in order to save her brother's life. In these modules, students read pertinent passages and explore issues presented in the text before examining congruent circumstances (not just involving sexual pressures) in contemporary life. Teachers and students find these interactions to be powerful, insightful, and supportive of class goals as teacher endorsements from the TOOJ website confirm:

> There are so many ways this workshop dovetails with skills students learn in class. How to ask questions, how to listen, how to respond respectfully, how to change their positions based on new information, etc. It is magical to witness, and a privilege to be able to frame and debrief the experience with students. Students learn real-world communication skills and learn to think outside of their own experiences.[15]

Students also offered positive responses to these classroom sessions. One student reported:

> From watching the videos I learned that Shakespeare isn't all about the fancy words and sonnets, but the stories encapsulate real social and human issues that people all around the world face so I must look at the plays trying to connect personally to what is going on in the story. Made me want to observe Shakespeare with a psychological lens since he tackles a lot of human and societal issues.[16]

Several students commented about their realization, through Shakespeare and conversation, that their preconceptions about those who are or were incarcerated did not conform to what they experienced through these sessions:

> I think it was a super valuable lesson, all parts of it. The stories were interesting, it was a bit outside our comfort zone which is great. I really enjoyed it. It was fascinating and eye-opening. It helped relate Shakespeare to real life.[17]

Sometimes, student participants in these modules have had experience with the criminal justice system through friends or family, but more commonly, these thoughtful and articulate FITs represent the young people's first encounter with someone who has experienced lengthy periods of incarceration.

One set of 2022 sessions initiated a collaboration between Lecturer Caroline Elizabeth Young at the University of Georgia (UGA), her students, and TOOJ members. Young is a gifted poet who teaches writing at UGA and in nearby prisons. These Zoom meetings facilitated even further exploration of the intersection between cognitive and affective learning that this chapter considers. In these sessions, after reading scenes from *Measure for Measure*, in an effort to connect Shakespeare with contemporary issues, the FITs shared original 'Prison Monologues' with the students, who both responded with analysis and then read out loud the TOOJ members' monologues to everyone present. Such intersections of personal writing with Shakespearean engagement is common in current Shakespeare and Prison programmes, particularly those working with young people, who may be surprised to learn that a number of prominent rap and hip hop artists, such as Tupac Shakur, have been significantly influenced by Shakespeare.

Young's students found the TOOJ compositions to be remarkable, as Evan Thomas explains about Amiti Bey's writing:

> Amiti Bey. A man who has a writing style unlike any other. His constant use of capitalized words and punctuation combined with his use of rhetorical techniques allows the reader to truly step into his shoes. The shoes of a man who faced twenty years of rejection and forty years of incarceration. A man who should not be nearly as positive thinking as he is. Yet when asked to write a monologue piece having to do with his time spent incarcerated, he chose to communicate a positive message. Surprised? Initially yes, but as my classmates and I got to know Bey, it would happen to very on brand.[18]

Another student, Akhila Kolluru, expresses the additional depth provided by having fellow classmates read the FITs' writings aloud:

> I thought I was emotionally prepared for a reading of Mohendra Singh's monologue 'The Irony of Life': I was wrong. A fellow UGA student read the piece with such feeling and empathy that it struck a chord with all who were listening. It was so moving that it felt like being introduced to the reading for the very first time. The pauses and inflections in her voice adds a new dimension to the piece, like it had been missing from the writing.[19]

Invariably, students acquire a renewed appreciation of the depth of understanding available through both the classic texts of Shakespeare and the contemporary presentations created by TOOJ participants.

Clearly, both incarcerated students and more typical students have a great deal to gain intellectually and emotionally from such collaborations. While we have progressed beyond the time when prisoners were not allowed to talk or see each other, however, the well-known pitfalls of what is called the Prison Industrial Complex still requires additional reform. Shakespeare in Prison programmes teach undergraduates and high schoolers about the corrections issues they will encounter as citizens and voters, at the same time that they learn in depth about Shakespeare. Incarcerated students learn that they can be part of widespread discussions about texts and issues with lengthy social, political, and intellectual pedigrees. Traditional students are often inspired by the dedication to education they see in the prisoners. And educated former prisoners move on to be impactful teachers and coaches. These are outcomes 'devoutly to be wished' (*Hamlet* 3.1).

Sheila T. Cavanagh is Professor of English at Emory University. Founding director of the World Shakespeare Project (*www.worldshakespeareproject.org*) and director of Emory's Year of Shakespeare (2016–2017), she was recently Fulbright/Global Shakespeare Distinguished Chair in the UK. Author of *Wanton Eyes and Chaste Desires: Female Sexuality in the Faerie Queene* (Indiana University Press, 1994) and *Cherished Torment: The Emotional Geography of Lady Mary Wroth's Urania* (Duquesne University Press, 2001) she has published widely in the fields of pedagogy and of Renaissance literature.

Steve Rowland is a documentary producer and director of Cultureworks Productions and Time Out of Joint (www.toj.org). A two-time Peabody Award winner, he is currently completing a documentary film, *Time out of Joint: Teaching Shakespeare in Prison*, focused on the Rehabilitation Through the Arts Shakespeare community at Woodbourne, NY Correctional Facility and prisoners' responses to Globe to Globe Festival films. A former instructor at Columbia University and Evergreen State College, he teaches Shakespeare at Monroe, WA Correctional Facility.

Notes

1. Stewart McLaughlin. *Behind Bars: A History of Wandsworth Prison* (London: Wandsworth Prison Museum, 2014) 3. Print.
2. Laura Bates. *Shakespeare Saved My Life: Ten Years in Solitary with the Bard*. (Naperville, Illinois: Sourcebooks, 2013). Print.
3. 'Half the Jails in England and Wales Causing Concern.' *The Times*, July 27. 2017. (https://www.thetimes.co.uk/edition/news/half-the-jails-in-england-and-wales-causing-concern-j965c0f9w). Web. Accessed 25 October 2018.
4. Many practitioners involved with Shakespeare in Prison efforts refer to incarcerated or formerly incarcerated students as 'returning' or 'returned' citizens, but this phrasing is not yet commonly understood.
5. TOOJ, in contrast, uses videoconferencing regularly.
6. Monroe Correctional Facility: 2013–2017. Student essays.
7. David R. Krathwohl, Benjamin S. Bloom, and Betram B. Masia. 1970. *Taxonomy of Educational Objectives: The Classification of Educational Goals. Handbook II: Affective Domain*. (London: Longman Group, 1970) Print.
8. *Taxonomy*, 96.

9. Hank Rogerson, *Shakespeare Behind Bars,* Philomath Films 2005. https://www.shakespearebehindbars.org/documentary/.
10. Curt Tofteland. 2017. Creating Circles of Trust. Course materials. Currently, these are referred to as 'Circles of Truth.'
11. Tofteland course materials, 5.
12. Tofteland course materials, 7.
13. Several of the RTA participants are now FITs in TOOJ (https://www.tooj.org/).
14. https://sites.msudenver.edu/tpswesternregion/.
15. https://www.tooj.org/teacher-endorsements.
16. https://www.tooj.org/testimonials.
17. https://www.tooj.org/testimonials.
18. University of Georgia student writings, 2022. These writings come from the TOOJ collaboration with Carolyn Elizabeth Young's class in 2022 and are included with the permission of the students.
19. University of Georgia student writings, 2022.

Chapter 6
Producing Space for Shakespeare

Rowan Mackenzie

Space has been accepted as a fundamental pillar to the disciplines of social science since the 1980s as many social changes are contextualised within the spatial environments in which they occur. Lefebvre's concepts of the creation of social space and the importance of the process of creating space serves well as a framework to consider the way in which space is both the physical entity where performance takes place and also the resultant mental and social capacity created by such activities. Of direct interest to my research is his concept of space being socially constructed and I will use this as a lens to consider how Shakespeare can enable those who are imprisoned in some way to create mental space within their confines or, indeed, to transcend the restrictive boundaries. Foucault's writing on the importance of space and the way in which it is used to embed power and control is particularly useful when considering the ways Shakespeare can create space for those incarcerated. Before we consider the way in which this takes effect it is important to define a number

Notes for this section begin on page 101.

of the theoretical terms used in the paper: space, reality, energy and time.

Foucault defines space as

> The space in which we live, which draws us out of ourselves, in which the erosion of our lives, our time and our history occurs, the space that claws and gnaws at us, is also, in itself, a heterogeneous space. ... we live inside a set of relations.[1]

Foucault divides space into utopias and heterotopias with utopias being unreal or imagined spaces whilst heterotopias are grounded in reality but possess the power to unsettle the expected.[2] These concepts are useful in considering the creation of space through the use of dramatic characters and how the imagined utopias can free people from the constraints of their existence but also symbiotically feed back into the expansion of that real space in which their lives are situated. I will also be drawing upon Lefebvre's assertion that 'physical space has no reality without the energy that is deployed within it'[3] in the comparison of physical spaces with those of a mental and social nature. He describes reality as the product of the three elements of the spatial triad which he articulates in *Critique of Everyday Life*.[4] His concept is that through the interaction of physical space, conceptual space and the resultant lived space in which social relations take place, reality is formed. This concept of reality as being something immediate, changeable and dependent on a combination of factors is one which resonates with my work. It also allows me to explore the way in which Shakespeare is therefore able to offer an alternative space for those whose current reality is restricted in some way.

It is also important to define 'energy'. Lefebvre describes

> time-space-energy. These three terms are necessary for describing and analysing cosmological reality. No single one suffice [...] Time and space without energy remain inert in the incomplete concept. Energy animates, reconnects, renders time and space conflictual.[5]

Energy in this context relates to movement, sound, social and emotional power which gives rise to something happening within space and time. Energy in the context of this chapter is of this definition: it can be the way in which a person occupies and manipulates a space either physically or emotionally. 'Power' has a dual meaning in that it can be both a positive force which gives people the ability to achieve or an oppressing force used to subdue others or to be subdued. Within the context of prisons there is an intrinsic dichotomy as arts and education projects seek to encourage personal empowerment but within the parameters of the prison regime.[6] The balance of power within prison can so easily be tipped through protests and violence which is something arts projects are mindful to avoid, although many of them do seek to challenge the system positively.

Foucault, in many of his writings challenges the efficacy of the prison system.

> Prisons do not diminish the crime rate: they can be extended, multiplied or transformed; the quantity of crime and criminals remains stable or, worse, increases.[7]

He argues that confining a large number of people in one place encourages them to create loyalties and a sense of community which in turn leads to them learning from each other about alternative ways to commit crimes. This links to the three main themes to his writing: dividing practices, scientific classification and subjectification,[8] mainly in the context of the division as prisoners are segregated from society both during their sentence and upon their release as the stigma of a criminal record is often socially and economically divisive. Foucault's theme of subjectification is one which I will also explore further in this chapter as offering people the opportunity to use Shakespeare does allow them to engage in self-formation and understanding which can in turn alter their perceptions and their belief in themselves.

Lefebvre's Marxist philosophy means that much of the focus of his writing is on the capitalist nature of modern society and the way in which social space is both constructed by this and also influences it. His articulation of class differences and the need for self-emancipation has relevance for the groups I work with and for whom I believe Shakespeare offers an alternative communication method: those who are marginalised by society through social and economic poverty, those with disabilities and mental health issues, and the homeless. The elements of Lefebvre's philosophical argument about the concept and production of space which resonate most strongly with my research relate to the idea that space cannot exist without the energy within it and that spaces are created and modified by the subjects within them. By engaging with Shakespeare within a confined space those involved are able to modify the space and their own sense of restriction. Edward W. Soja argues in *Postmodern Geographies* that 'space is not a scientific object removed from ideology and politics [...] Space has been shaped and moulded from historical and natural elements.'[9]

This chapter explores the extent to which the space of a prison is affected by the Shakespeare activities performed within it and Lefebvre's spatial triad as well as considering the ways in which the use of Shakespeare is self-formative in the context of Foucault's subjectification. The primary case-study is an *Othello* session with a group of men in a local, remand prison, where there is a high turn-over of men awaiting trial or serving short custodial sentences. Considering firstly the prison within the context of first or natural space[10] and the physical locale; the design focus for any prison is containment and control as evidenced by the locked gates, razor wire and uniformed officers. The prison where this work took place was built two centuries ago and the exterior closely resembles a castle. The first session I facilitated there was in October 2017 as part of the two-week prison-wide Talent Unlocked Arts Festival, endorsed by the Governing Governor.

The session was attended by 12 men and was held in the prison library, a somewhat cramped space to facilitate such an event, especially as the library was essentially two small interlinked rooms. There were no windows in this entirely internal room, lined with floor to ceiling bookcases. We managed to squeeze in a flipchart and arrange sufficient chairs to accommodate the men in a rough circle in one of the two rooms. They began to arrive individually as the librarian sought them out and sent them in from the wing. I introduced myself to each with a handshake as they arrived and asked for their first names. It was clear that few of them knew each other and the feeling at the start of the session was not that of a cohesive group but of a random collection of strangers who felt they were waiting to be 'instructed' on Shakespeare. The physical space (or lack thereof) and poor layout also influenced the feeling within the room; there was insufficient space for the men to greet each other even if they wanted to and the circle was misshapen to fit the spatial confines. As the room filled up the atmosphere was muted with few of them choosing to speak to each other beyond initial greetings across the room.

I had chosen to work on *Othello* 3.3 with a heavily edited version of the conversation between Othello and Iago; focusing on how Iago poisons Othello's mind against Desdemona.[11] I had chosen this scene because I thought that themes of jealousy and concerns about infidelity would resonate with these men, many of whom who were currently away from their partners. After a brief synopsis of the plot up to 3.3 we had an initial read through of the script I provided, which showed the variance in their confidence and their reading levels with some of the men reading only a word or two whilst others confidently read whole speeches. The conceived space here still felt like a prison location: a tiny library where there were interruptions by people wanting to loan or return books. There was little doubt that this was a functional part of the prison and not somewhere where the imagination could soar and the confines be forgotten, as I asked them to prepare to adapt the script into modern language. The men were split into two groups (a decision partially driven by the physical constraints of the space we were in as trying to work as a single group would have been difficult in such confined quarters).

One group elected to be Othello and the other to be Iago; each was equipped with flipchart paper and pens and tasked with rewriting the edited script into the language they would themselves use if they were having this conversation with a close friend. They arranged themselves in more natural groupings, one group in each room, and started to look at their lines. Initially, they sought guidance from me as to what they should be writing as though there was a right or wrong translation into modern language[12] but as they became more involved and started to think about what the characters were saying they started to form their own opinions and to discuss them within the group. This change in focus from wanting my approval and recognition to expressing their view for group consideration was a fundamental one and to me it transformed the space they were in; this became Lefebvre's social space where the space is a 'tool of thought and of action.'[13] For this brief period of time, these were not imprisoned men, they were individuals discussing human nature and how people react to love and perceived betrayal. Through the use of Shakespeare's characters and plot they were able to engage as human beings not prisoners and inhabit a lived, social space which appeared to offer them equality to each other and to me. The men were debating the meaning of the line 'I do not think but Desdemona's honest' (3.3.229) and whilst they asked my opinion they were soon throwing in their own alternative suggestions of Othello's mental state.

Using Lefebvre's spatial triad as a model; the physical and the conceptual space within the prison gave a lived space with a feeling of restraint and confinement. There was no possibility of alteration to the physical and conceived spaces to change the final element of the triad. The introduction of Shakespeare, altered the physical and conceived spaces significantly and allowed the men to change this from a space of restriction into one where they were able to freely discuss ideas. In the subsequent five years of working in prisons facilitating Shakespeare this is a phenomenon I have witnessed countless times with many different groups and individuals It is this alteration which is the catalyst for a change in the spatial realm, the group dynamic and which may allow them to consider future changes (should they choose to do so).[14] It is in this respect that Foucault's subjectification is appropriate to consider here, examining how and why the men may have chosen to consider potential changes to themselves.[15] However, a note of caution here, there is no expectation of people experiencing some kind of epiphany and altering their lives from a two-hour workshop. Even within a much longer-term project such as those undertaken in Borallon Training and Correctional Centre by Queensland Shakespeare Ensemble the expectation is often not for fundamental change but to provide some enjoyment and creativity amidst the monotony of prison life.[16] There are examples where people have had their lives altered by engagement in a prison arts project (whether that be Shakespeare, theatre, music or visual art)[17] but in many cases it is the creation of a space which is not imbued with a feeling of incarceration which may be the benefit of any type of prison arts.[18] Having now facilitated long-term collaborative theatre companies for a number of years in two prisons I have personally seen people experience both ends of this spectrum of impact – some will primarily simply enjoy the rehearsals as a respite from the monotony of the prison regime whilst others will harness the opportunity to reflect on themselves through the medium of 'dramatic distancing' in relation to the characters they have enacted.[19]

If we consider the impact of subjectification and Foucault's explanation that it is around self-formation and change, often guided by an external authority figure,[20] there are interesting ways to read the 2017 *Othello* session which may give some insight into how the men responded. At the outset of the session a couple of them asked for permission to return to their cells for various reasons; which I was told is common for these type of group activities. These requests were soon forgotten as they became more involved in the session and started to contribute. One particularly notable example was the man who had asked to leave at the start but was then collected to attend a clinic appointment and when the officers arrived for him he was concerned about missing the rest of the session and agreed to go only when they assured him that the wait time was minimal and he could return to the library straight afterwards. Thankfully, he returned to the group just as we began our read-through of their scripts and he was pleased to be able to be involved with the final outputs.

The adaptation into contemporary colloquial language gave the men the opportunity to make Shakespeare their own; through them owning the words they used in the mini-performance at the end.

> Man does not live by words alone; all subjects are situated in a space in which they must either recognise themselves or lose themselves, a space which they may both enjoy and modify.[21]

Lefebvre's description of how we interact with language and space resonates strongly in the context of prison. Shakespeare's words were the starting point for this session but they enabled the men to take control of the language themselves and adapt them into phrases which have more direct and personal meaning to the lives they are living and the interactions they have with their friends and enemies.[22] For many people, words can be seen as a barrier, marking them out from society if they do not have high literacy skills or an extensive vocabulary. Additionally, trauma can often reduce or remove an individual's ability to articulate their experiences and leave them feeling frustrated about their disconnection from language. This can impact on their confidence and their ability to be accepted by others, especially those in positions of authority.

One would expect that Shakespeare's language with all its complexities and the inherent cultural capital of his work would be even more pronounced in the way it does this. Traditionally Shakespeare has been seen as belonging to those with higher academic and social education. Sharon O'Dair argues in *Class, Critics and Shakespeare* that this needs to be subverted but it currently remains so for many people. O'Dair argues that the connection between education and both occupational opportunity and cultural capital needs to be weakened to foster a less stratified society and protect the 'freedom to do intellectually challenging work.'[23] I accept that for many people Shakespeare is seen as culturally upper-class, but this opinion is not founded on any basis of evidence from Shakespeare's own life or the plays. He wrote plays to attract people into his theatre in a time when theatres often shared their spaces with bear-baiting and were an entertainment of a similar level to these and to brothels.[24] He did not write solely for the highly educated and many of his plays are filled with bawdy humour from characters such as Falstaff, Mistress Quickly and Doll Tearsheet. Shakespeare created characters across all echelons of society, from royalty to paupers and his work can appeal to anyone with any literacy level and any academic ability.

Shakespeare created characters which epitomise Lefebvre's description of space as something in which people 'must either recognise themselves or lose themselves'[25] and it is these characters which enable people to explore alternative lives which they would not have accessed otherwise. By enabling someone to consider Iago's drivers for making Othello doubt Desdemona we allow them to consider the negative aspects of their own personality but without forcing them to openly disclose them.[26] Therapy requires an individual to discuss their own inner-thoughts and personality in order to challenge these and look at ways to re-engineer brain pathways. Improvisational theatre of the kind facilitated in prisons by Geese Theatre and other companies offers this therapeutic opportunity but one step removed via the use of characters and masks; a concept underpinned by cognitive behavioural therapy and role theory. The improvisations are built around how the individuals respond to situations which are likely to incite their anger or aggression and the group then explore alternative resolutions.[27] Augusto Boal expressed his frustration at the way in which prisoners seem to be unable to imagine alternative narratives and instead view themselves as the oppressed in all situations.[28]

The use of text rather than improvisation allows the participants not only to consider but to also physically verbalise a different narrative, to speak in a voice other than their own. By assuming the role of a scripted character an individual is empowered to speak and, in turn think, in ways which their previously self-limiting beliefs may not have allowed. This enables them to expand into the space they occupy more freely and, at times, transcend the boundaries they may feel are imposed on them. The focus is on drama not therapy but the text enables people to become emotionally engaged with the character and their decisions.[29] For people who struggle to be analytical and wholly rational about their own strengths and weaknesses (as many of us would admit to) the use of a pre-defined character offers opportunities to assess and understand parts of our own psyche which may otherwise be too painful to consider. It also allows an individual to understand multiple perspectives of the issue. When taking the role of Iago the men in the workshop, without prompting from me as the facilitator, considered why he was so filled with hatred and whether that was aimed at Othello, Desdemona or others in general. We had discussions around the potential motivations for his bitterness: had Othello been involved with Iago's wife, was he angry at Othello's promotion above him, was he racist?[30] J.I.M. Stewart argues that 'Iago is a device of Othello's by which Othello hears an inner force which he would fain hear and fain deny'[31] and if we follow this line of thinking then Iago is the internal devil to Othello, voicing the suspicions which would otherwise be unseemly in such a noble man.

Using Shakespeare in this context is not an attempt at therapy but it does allow the participants to engage with these questions at a deeper level if they should choose to do so. Her Majesty's Prison and Probate Services (HMPPS) National Research Council approved me undertaking of Shakespeare projects in multiple prisons considering the way in which the work enables those involved to contemplate their personalities in connection with the characters and to what extent it may allow them to move towards therapy.[32] These projects allow them to interact on a superficial level with the activity – i.e. something which offers them an alternative to their cells and gives them some interaction with a person outside of their normal circle of exposure within the prison (and the importance of this itself should not be underestimated). It allows them to use their imaginations and transcend the walls of the prison for a period of time as they reflect on when they have felt jealous or betrayed both in prison and prior to conviction. They can for a while be contained within the prison physically but mentally outside of that confined space. And, for those who want to, they can consider the deeper implications for themselves and others of the behaviour and motivations of the characters.[33] The psychology of Othello and Iago has interested academics for decades and the history of this is well summarised in Michael Jacobs' *Shakespeare on the Couch* which dedicates a chapter to the jealousy of both Othello and Leontes.[34]

The space in the prison library became not just two small rooms but instead opened up to allow the men to discuss their personal fears of being cuckolded whilst they are imprisoned,[35] discuss the ways in which the tale of Othello echoes a similar folklore story in other countries where the two men are brothers not friends[36] in which Shakespeare's multi-layered language in many ways resembles the layers of nuanced meaning contained within Sanskrit writings.[37] The characters of Othello and Iago allowed the men to both recognize elements of themselves and also lose themselves in the stage-play world for the duration of the session. They transformed over a short period of time from prisoners seeking approval from the figure of authority running the session to a unified group debating the meaning of the line 'I do not think but Desdemona's honest' (3.3.229). The group working on Othello's speeches believed this line to be pivotal in the scene and to have multiple meanings, ranging from his self-reassurance that his wife is truthful to a more philosophical view that if she was false he would cease to be able to think or function. The educational level of the men involved was not relevant to this workshop and did not impede them from engaging with the text. Every person in that session had a valid contribution to make as to the exact meaning of the script but no-one, including myself, has the definitive answer.

In 2021 one of the collaborative theatre companies I facilitate in prison (Emergency Shakespeare) performed a production of *Othello* and the actors in this company drew heavily on their own experiences of relationships, friendships, jealousy and anger when they worked on their characterisation of the roles.[38] Interestingly the actors playing Othello and Iago were cell-mates and so the dynamic of their friendship in real-life gave an additional poignancy to the way in which Iago betrays those who trust him. The actor who played Iago chose to do so to address some personal demons relating to his index offence and his behaviour and attitude around the time his crime was committed. He and I discussed this in depth on several occasions and I played the role of Emilia to offer support as he worked through the areas he felt most traumatic. Throughout the process he kept detailed journals which allowed him to process his emotions and thoughts and these were then discussed both with myself and his therapist. Following the performances he spoke of the relief he felt at having faced this significant challenge and the way it had enabled him to confirm that he had moved beyond the identity he had at the time of the offence; supporting the 'new me' model he had worked on through Kaizen, his Offender Behaviour Programme.[39]

Despite the inherent cultural capital of Shakespeare there is something which transcends traditional education and literacy and which appeals to our inner core of humanity. It is not necessary to have a deep academic grasp of language, whether oral or written, in order to identify with the characters. As Cicely Berry argues, the universal appeal of Shakespeare is because he 'didn't dumb his plays down in any way, but found a way through language to engage the educated and the uneducated alike'.[40] This was certainly the case in the workshop I was delivering; I have no knowledge of the educational level of the participants but even for those for whom English was not a first language the characters offered something they identified with and wanted to explore.

This space we created during the workshop was, as Lefebvre describes, 'a tool of thought and of action'[41] which prompted the men to have interest in something outside of their own circle of engagement (which in prison is often restricted to the wing, the yard and personal interests such as sport). However, in the context of creating space for Shakespeare, Lefebvre's description of that space as a 'means of control, and hence of domination, of power' is a point I would dispute. This creation of mental space for prisoners is, if anything, a subversion of the traditional power structure in prison; it allows them to free themselves from some of the rules imposed upon them and whilst they are not physically free they have a mental freedom made available to them that was not previously there. Shakespeare allows these prisoners what one of them describes in Laura Bates' work as 'an alternative outlet',[42] one which gives them an ability to release anger, frustration and revenge without resorting to physical violence. Tom Magill describes how 'destructive anger can be transformed into creativity. We just need someone to believe in us at the right moment for it to happen'[43] and this is precisely the space that can be created to enable a person to flourish.

I am not claiming that this work (or even the longer term projects which have enabled me to conduct ethnographic research over a period of several years) results in an epiphany for all of those involved, leaving them substantially changed from reading Shakespeare. Such a claim would be simplistic and ignore the sheer variances of human nature. There is no accurate way to assess the way in which each person is altered by such engagement as we are all individuals who react to stimuli differently and we are all on our own journey, influenced by our own set of experiences.[44] This challenge of measuring the success is one which is being wrestled with by academics and practitioners and in a world where funding is often outcome focused it is one where progress needs to be made, however, there does not appear to be any easy solution.[45] The creation of space for Shakespeare is evident in the way in which a group of disparate prisoners of multiple ethnicities engaged in a philosophical debate about love, friendship, jealousy and betrayal. During the few hours of the workshop they began to show increased confidence, engagement in learning practices, cooperation with fellow inmates and demonstrated independence of thought and activity. These skills are transferable outside of the workshop and are necessary for many of them to consider changing their situation during their sentence and upon subsequent release.

Lefebvre's concept of space as being something which both contains and is expanded by the activity within it is one which resonates with my overall hypothesis that creating space for Shakespeare in the lives of those for whom communication is difficult enables them to expand the space in which they live and this gives them more opportunities. Whether those opportunities are as life-changing as choosing not to reoffend again or as simple as the ability to see a mythical land in our imagination may not be important. That it gives individuals and groups the opportunity to experience more than they otherwise could makes it valuable regardless of the changes it may engender. Through this creation of social space where everyone is engaged people have the opportunity to transcend the confines which have previously restricted them, even if only for a short period. As my longer-term research also evidences, this type of activity has multiple benefits: increased confidence, opportunity to engage both intellectually and emotionally, social interaction with those outside the current social circle, consideration of the choices one has in life when situations arise and the ability to empathize and articulate a point of view other than their own.

To acknowledge a valid point raised by Governor Novis, it does not have to be Shakespeare which has this effect,[46] but for many of the men I have been working with Shakespeare opens doors which may previously have seemed locked. I maintain that Shakespeare offers a multi-layered benefit through the alternative narratives it provides and the cultural capital it carries which often challenges the external world's perception of prisoners who engages with the Bard's work. However, I do accept that it will not appeal to everyone and for some an alternative creative outlet is more appropriate. However, if we can deepen our understanding of how Shakespeare creates space for those who choose to engage with it then we can facilitate this space to enable those incarcerated by physical or mental boundaries being able to influence and proactively create more positive social space in which they and the community can thrive.

OTHELLO	***OTHELLO – TALENT UNLOCKED***
OTHELLO Excellent wretch! Perdition catch my soul But I do love thee! And when I love thee not Chaos is come again.	OTHELLO She's a good woman. She caught my soul, and I do love her. When I am not with her my life is in chaos.
IAGO My noble lord –	IAGO Hmmm?
OTHELLO What dost thou say Iago?	OTHELLO Why are you saying that?
IAGO Did Michael Cassio, when you wooed my lady, Know of your love?	IAGO When you were chatting up your lady, did Michael Cassio know of your love?
OTHELLO He did, from first to last. Why dost thou ask? Is he not honest?	OTHELLO Yes, he did completely. Why do you ask?
IAGO Honest, my lord?	IAGO Am I supposed to know?
OTHELLO Honest? Aye, honest.	OTHELLO Why do you ask? Why, is he lying?
IAGO My lord, for aught I know.	IAGO Am I supposed to know?
OTHELLO Though dost mean something, I heard thee say even now thou lik'st not that When Cassio left my wife: what didst not like? If thou dost love me show me thy thought.	OTHELLO What does it mean; it does mean something.

OTHELLO

IAGO
I dare be sworn, I think, that he is honest.

OTHELLO
Nay, yet there's more in this:
I prithee speak to me, as to thy thinkings,
As thou dost ruminate, and give thy worst of thoughts
The worst of words.

IAGO
I do beseech you,
It were not for your quiet nor your good
Nor for my manhood, honesty and wisdom.

OTHELLO
By heavens I'll know thy thoughts!

IAGO
Oh beware, my lord, of jealousy!
It is the green-eyed monster, which doth mock
The meat it feeds on. That cuckold lives in bliss
Who, certain of his fate, loves not his wronger,
But O, what damned minutes tells he o'er
Who dotes yet doubts, suspects yet strongly loves!

OTHELLO – TALENT UNLOCKED

IAGO
Don't make me swear on it, but I think he is honest.

OTHELLO
What are you saying? You seen them talking, wo what don't you like about that? If you're my friend tell me what you're thinking.

IAGO
Honestly mate, if it weren't for the fact that you are a nice bloke, I wouldn't tell you my thoughts.
And, because it would
To let you know my thoughts.

OTHELLO
So, there is more to it. Please tell me what you're thinking. Don't hold back, tell me.

IAGO
Beware of jealousy, it eats you alive. If you don't love her it doesn't really matter but if you love her and still doubt her it will do your head in

OTHELLO

OTHELLO
Oh misery!
Tis not to make me jealous
To say my wife is fair, feeds well, loves company,
Is free of speech, sings, plays and dances well.
I'll see before I doubt, when I doubt, prove,
And on the proof there is no more but this:
Away at once with love or jealousy!

IAGO
Look to your wife, observe her well with Cassio.
Wear your eyes thus, not jealous nor secure.
I hope you will consider what is spoke
Comes from my love. But I do see you're moved;
I am to pray you not to strain my speech
To grosser issues nor to larger reach
Than to suspicion.

OTHELLO
I do not think but Desdemona's honest.

IAGO
Long live she so; and long live you to think so.

OTHELLO
And yet how nature, erring from itself –
bring into question my manhood, honesty and wisdom.
If more thou dost perceive, let me know more:
Set on thy wife to observe. Leave me Iago.

OTHELLO – TALENT UNLOCKED

OTHELLO
What the fuck man, are you sure? Well I am not jealous, I trust my wife, she speaks her mind. We have a good life together and I am not going to doubt her until there is proof. There really is none at the moment so for now I am not going to be jealous.

IAGO
Watch your wife when she is with Cassio, and go with what you see and not what you are already thinking. Bear in mind my words to you are from a loving place. I can see you're affected so please don't read too much into my words.

OTHELLO
I do not think so, I do believe my wife is honest.

IAGO
I hope she stays honest.....and I hope you keep thinking it.

OTHELLO
Ok, maybe life is like that at times, nature does do crazy things from time to time. If you think there is more to it ask your wife to keep an eye on her. Go now, leave me be.

OTHELLO

IAGO
My lord, I take my leave.

OTHELLO
Why did I marry?
This honest creature doubtless
Sees and knows more – much more – than he unfolds.
This fellow's of exceeding honesty
And knows all qualities, with a learned spirit,
Of human dealings. If I do prove her haggard,
Thou that her jesses were my dear heart-strings,
I'd whistle her off and let her down the wind
To prey at fortune.
She's gone, I am abused, and my relief
Must be to loathe her. O curse of marriage
That we can call these delicate creatures ours
And not their appetites! I had rather be a toad
And live upon the vapour of a dungeon
Than keep a corner in the thing I love
For other's uses. Look where she comes:
If she be false, O then heaven mocks itself,
I'll not believe't.

OTHELLO – TALENT UNLOCKED

IAGO
Alright, I'm leaving

OTHELLO
Why did I marry?
This honest friend of mine knows more than what he is telling me. I do believe he is looking out for me as a true friend would. He's very honest, he knows about life, he knows the score.
If I do prove her wrong and find out she has been cheating I will let go of her and throw her to the wolves, to hell with her.
It's over, she's burnt my head out, I now hate her, why did I marry her? She is a lovely girl but why did I not see her lust? To be cheated on is as low as can be when ones in love. I'd rather be single knowing I've had a piece of her.
Look where she is now. HA!

The passage above is the modern translation the men involved in the workshop produced of this edited scene, replacing Shakespeare's language with their own vernacular. This exercise gave them a sense of ownership of the scene and enabled them to use it as a refraction of how they themselves would feel in similar circumstances; combining Shakespeare with their own life experiences in a powerful heterotopia.

Rowan Mackenzie is both practitioner and academic, working with specialised communities. Her doctoral research used spatial theory as a framework to examine global theatre practices with incarcerated people and people with mental health issues, learning disabilities and experiences of homelessness. She is founder and Artistic Director of Shakespeare UnBard, which facilitates collaborative theatre companies in a number of UK prisons, and Co-Chair of the Shakespeare Beyond Borders Alliance. She is the recipient of many national and international awards for her work, including the prestigious Butler Trust award. She has published numerous chapters and essays on Shakespeare within prisons, Shakespeare with learning-disabled actors and the heterotopic potential of applied theatre. Her monograph *Creating Space for Shakespeare* was published by Bloomsbury Arden in March 2023.

Notes

1. Michel Foucault, 'Of other spaces: Utopias and Heteretopias', *Architecture / Mouvement / Continuité October*, 1984, ("Des Espace Autres," a lecture given by Michael Foucault in March 1967 Translated from the French by Jay Miskowiec).
2. Peter Johnson articulates Foucault's six principles of heterotopias as being that they
    - become established in all cultures but in diverse forms (especially as sites of 'crisis' or later 'deviation').
    - mutate and have specific operations at different points in history.
    - juxtapose in a single space several incompatible spatial elements.
    - encapsulate spatio-temporal discontinuities or intensities.
    - presuppose an ambivalent system of opening/closing, entry/exit, distance/penetration.
    - have a specific operation in relation to other spaces as, for example, illusion or compensation on his website *Heterotopian Studies* http://www.heterotopiastudies.com/whats-it-about/ (accessed 20 August 2018).
3. Henri Lefebvre, *The Production of Space* (translated by Donald Nicholson Smith), (Oxford and Victoria: Blackwell Publishing, 1991) p.13.
4. Henri Lefebvre, *Critique of Everyday Life: The One Volume Edition* (translated by John Moore), London and New York: Verso, 2014). Lefebvre uses the spatial triad to describe three types of space: Representational /perceived space which is the physical space surrounding us, Representations of space /conceived space which is the conceptual and Spatial practice /lived space in which social relations take place. Spatial practice is created by the way in which the first two play out and reality is created through the interaction of all of the elements of the spatial triad.

5. Henri Lefebvre, *Rhythmanalysis: Space, Time and Everyday Life*, (translated by Stuart Elden and Gerald Moore), (London and New York: Continuum, 2004) p.60.
6. The vision and mission statements of many applied theatre companies articulate their desire to enhance life skills, encourage learning and open up new opportunities to their participants. Examples include, but are not limited to, Shakespeare Behind Bars https://www.shakespearebehindbars.org/about/mission/ [accessed 28 August 2018], Clean Break http://www.cleanbreak.org.uk/about/ [accessed 28 August 2018] and TIPP https://www.tipp.org.uk/our-vision/ [accessed 28 August 2018].
7. Michel Foucault, *Discipline and Punish: The birth of the prison*, (translated by Alan Sherridan), (London and New York: Penguin Books, 1977) p.265.
8. Paul Rabinow (ed.), *The Foucault Reader* (London and New York: Penguin Books, 1984), describes in his introduction the three main elements to Foucault's work:
    - Dividing practices (lepers/poor/insane/prisons/psychiatric units/sexual deviants) 'essentially "dividing practices" are modes of manipulation that combine the mediation of a science (or pseudo-science) and the practice of exclusion – usually in a spatial sense but always in a social one.' These are techniques of domination.
    - Scientific classification – how disciplines achieve internal autonomy but how the disciplines which we use to make sense of life and power have changed abruptly at certain times. He sees discourse as linked to the social practices and doesn't approve of trying to find a deeper discourse. He's interested in the shifting ways the body and social institutions related to it are interlinked. The body was often treated as an object in clinics in 19th century – this links to both dividing practices and scientific classification.
    - Subjectification – the way in which a human turns themselves into a subject. Here the person is actively engaged in self-formation (not the passive recipient). The person undergoes change through a process of self-understanding, aided by an external authority figure.
9. Edward W. Soja, *Postmodern Geographies: The Reassertion of Space in Critical Social Theory*, (London and New York: Verso, 1989) p.80.
10. Henri Lefebvre, *The Production of Space* (translated by Donald Nicholson-Smith), (Oxford and Victoria: Blackwell Publishing, 1991) p.11–14.
11. William Shakespeare, *Othello* (ed. E.A.J. Honigman), (London: Arden Shakespeare, 1995).
12. During a meeting with Paul Johnston, Cluster Head of Learning, Skills and Employment HMP Leicester and HMP Gartree on 18th October 2017 following him observing my session he commented on the way in which inmates usually struggle with group activities and instead want one to one attention from the teacher. He explained that this is an ongoing issue which teachers in prisons face and that he anticipated that the same issues would arise in the *Othello* session but that he had been surprised to see how they had instead started to seek feedback from each other and build on ideas from the group.

13. Henri Lefebvre, *The Production of Space* (translated by Donald Nicholson Smith), (Oxford and Victoria: Blackwell Publishing, 1991) p.26.
14. At the end of the session, during the short debrief a number of them commented that they wanted to be involved in more such sessions. Governor Phil Novis discussed the importance of engaging the men in any kind of learning activity as mainstream education often holds little appeal for them but engagement in developing life-skills can make a significant difference to their future prospects upon release from prison. Discussed during a conversation with Novis after a Shakespeare workshop at HMP Leicester 1 June 2018.
15. As above, the debrief session gave the men the opportunity to ask for further sessions of this kind. Following a later workshop at HMP Leicester on *Macbeth* 1 June 2018 the men requested the opportunity to try some acting and this led to getting Governor Novis' approval to run an additional workshop 20 June 2018, at the request of the men wanting to improve their speaking and acting skills – a proactive request from men who often demonstrate only reactivity and passivity within a prison environment. Feedback questionnaires gathered from these *Macbeth* sessions noted improvements in 'empathy', 'listening skills', 'writing skills' and 'public speaking' – all of which are transferrable skills which the men can use during their sentence and upon release.
16. Rob Pensalfini, Artistic Director of Queensland Shakespeare Ensemble and Director of the Shakespeare Prison Project which works in Borallon Training and Correctional Centre described to me that he does not always expect to alter the lives of many of the men he works with in any long-term, fundamental way. Instead, he aims to provide them with some creative outlet and produce an interesting piece of theatre. Discussed in person during the Shakespeare in Prisons Conference 2018, San Diego, USA, 22–25 March 2018.
17. Sammy Byron attributes much of his current positive lifestyle to the programmes he undertook with Shakespeare Behind Bars whilst incarcerated in the US. Discussed in person during the Shakespeare in Prisons Conference 2018, San Diego, USA, 22–25 March 2018 and also discussed in the film documentary *Shakespeare Behind Bars*, (dir. Hank Rogerson), (Philomath films, 2006).
18. Aixa Takkal, Katarina Horrox and Alberto Rubio-Garrido, 'The issue of space in a prison art therapy group: a reflection through Martin Heidegger's conceptual frame', *International Journal of Art Therapy 23.2*, pp.136–142. Discusses the use of space and time for a prison visual arts therapy session and how this impacts on the participant's view of the activities.
19. Sue Jennings, *Dramatherapy: Theory and Practice*, Volume 2 (London: Routledge, 1992) p.17
20. Michel Foucault, 'Afterword: The Subject and Power' in Hubert L. Dreyfus and Paul Rabinow, *Michel Foucault: Beyond Structuralism and Hermeneutics* (Oxon and New York: Routledge, 2013) pp. 224–246.
21. Henri Lefebvre, *The Production of Space* (translated by Donald Nicholson-Smith), (Oxford and Victoria: Blackwell Publishing, 1991) p.35.

104 *Rowan Mackenzie*

22. During the session at HMP Leicester the men created lines such as 'if you're my friend tell me what you're thinking', 'so there is more to it, don't hold back, tell me' and 'he's very honest, he knows about life, he knows the score' spoken by Othello in 3.3. These lines resonated with them and were how they would speak to their own friends about this subject of friendship and suspected betrayal. The exercise encouraged them to consider how they articulate their thoughts and to work together as a group to reach a consensus.
23. Sharon O'Dair *Class, Critics and Shakespeare: bottom lines on the culture wars* (Ann Arbour: University of Michigan Press, 2000) p. 4.
24. Andreas Höfele, *Stage, Stake and Scaffold,* (Oxford: Oxford University Press, 2011) describes the close physical and cultural links between theatres and bear-baiting sites such as the Bear Garden in Renaissance London. Steven Mullaney, *The Place of the Stage: License, Play and Power in Renaissance England* (Chicago: University of Chicago Press, 1988), p.22.
25. Henri Lefebvre, *The Production of Space* (translated by Donald Nicholson Smith), (Oxford and Victoria: Blackwell Publishing, 1991) p. 35.
26. During the session at HMP Leicester the men created lines such as 'If I do prove her wrong and find out she's been cheating I will let go of her and throw her to the wolves, to hell with her' which came from group discussion about how they would feel to be cheated on romantically. Many of the men made comment about how angry and violent this would make them feel but as a group they chose to articulate their feelings with the metaphor of 'wolves' rather than any implicit to reference to them inflicting violence on either party.
27. Interview with Emma Smallman, Facilitator at Geese Theatre, 25 March 2016 where she explained their work using masks (typically of a joker, a brick wall, 'poor little me', angry fist, the rescuer and Mr Cool) and then asking participants to respond to the person in the centre who is wearing a mask to signify their emotion at that time. Geese Theatre is very active and focuses on making people experience the emotion and then unpicking what the triggers were to make that emotion flare before then considering how a reoccurrence of this can be avoided or managed. Smallman explained that in Geese Theatre 'the work is therapeutic but not therapy'.
28. Jonathan Shailor *Performing New Lives: Prison Theatre* (London and Philadelphia: Jessica Kingsley Publishers, 2011) p. 182.
29. During the session at HMP Leicester the men discussed how they would feel if their trusted best friend told them their new partner was being unfaithful, the conversation included them being unwilling to believe it but trusting their best friend implicitly and the anger they would feel towards the partner and the person she was involved with. No details were requested from the men but some of them did use phrases such as 'I was so angry' suggesting they were recalling lived experiences rather than from imagining the plight of Othello and Desdemona.
30. The session had been set up for the men to adapt the edited text from 3.3 into their own language and this triggered conversations between them about what the lines meant intellectually but also the emotions which were being represented and the motivations for the characters. They treated the characters as though they were real people and this high level of engagement did bring them to life within the space where we were working.

31. J.I.M. Stewart *Character and Motive in Shakespeare* (London: Longman, 1949) p.103.
32. HMPPS NRC Approval Reference 2018-065, granted 14th March 2018. The approval letter confirms that 'The Committee does approve the following research questions and methods.

    Questions
    - Does this type of project offer a stepping stone towards therapy for some participants?
    - How does the involvement in a workshop enable participants to consider their own personalities and behaviour in relation to the dramatic characters they are engaging with?

    Methods
    - Data collection via questionnaires, semi-structured interviews, and observations of the sessions.'
33. The adaptation of Othello's speeches into lines such as 'It's over, she's burnt my head out, I now hate her, why did I marry her' was imbued with a sense of personal experience of loss and betrayal. We did not explore formally any details of their own experience of this situation but a number of the men mentioned how angry and betrayed they had felt rather than how they would imagine Othello to feel and this use of the first person suggested it had resonated personally with them.
34. Michael Jacobs, *Shakespeare on the Couch* (London: Karnac Books Ltd, 2008) pp. 11–26.
35. A number of the men volunteered their thoughts on how they would feel if their partners were unfaithful whilst they are in prison and the fear that this could be happening. This was not instigated as part of the session but did come up in discussion, albeit at a relatively light-touch level, i.e., 'I'd hate her', 'mine wouldn't do that to me' rather than any deeper personal revelations of experiences or private concerns.
36. One of the discussions held during the *Othello* workshop was a folk tale in Sanskrit which has a similar plotline to *Othello* but where the two men are brothers not friends. This was deemed by some men to make the story more plausible as they felt that the blood connection gave credence to Othello's belief of Iago's poisonous lies.
37. Sanskrit is an ancient language used widely across Hinduism, Jainism, Buddhism and other religious cultures. It is layered with encoded meanings and the Sanskrit readers (4 of the 12 attendees) in the *Othello* workshop discussed how this richly layered language resembles the language used by Shakespeare which too is filled with meanings and can be understood at multiple levels.
38. Emergency Shakespeare is based in a Category C prison for men convicted of sexual offences; founded in 2019 it comprises of myself and 15 actors at any one time and to date has performed a number of productions for other prisoners and families to attend.
39. Kaizen is an accredited Offender Behaviour Programme for men classified as high or very high risk and who have been convicted of violent or sexual offences, https://www.gov.uk/guidance/offending-behaviour-programmes-and-interventions [accessed 30 September 2022]

106 Rowan Mackenzie

40. Cicely Berry of the Royal Shakespeare Company was one of the forerunners of prison Shakespeare and delivered workshops in prisons between 1982 and 1986. Rob Pensalfini, *Prison Shakespeare: For these deep shames and great indignities*, (Basingstoke and New York: Palgrave Macmillan, 2016) p.17 quoted Cicely Berry's response to those who challenge prisoner's ability to grasp Shakespeare and make it authentically their own.
41. Lefebvre p.26.
42. Laura Bates, *Shakespeare Saved My Life: Ten years in solitary with the Bard*, (Illinois: Sourcebooks Inc. 2013) p.181.
43. Tom Magill, Artistic Director of the Educational Shakespeare Company (ESC), *Release from Rage*, Magill's backstory about his own time in prison, published on ESC's website http://esc-film.com/release-from-rage/ [accessed 18 June 2018].
44. Bridget Keehan 'Theatre, Prison and Rehabilitation: new narratives of purpose?' *Research in Drama Education: The Journal of Applied Theatre and Performance Vol. 20, No. 3*, 2015, pp. 391–394 describes the challenges of assessing the impact of drama initiatives on those incarcerated but the importance of projects considering how best to analyse these impacts. https://doi.org/10.1080/13569783.2015.1060118 [accessed 21 July 2018].
45. Michael Balfour speaking during panel session *Gathering the Data: Evaluation and Research* at the Shakespeare in Prisons Conference, The Old Globe, San Diego, March 2018, where he described the Griffiths University research project *Captive Audiences: The impact of performing arts projects in Australian prisons*, which was carried out between 2012 and 2014 and where he discussed the 'real need to map ourselves onto the institutional map' but acknowledged the challenges of understanding and quantifying exactly how and why these projects have an impact.
46. Phil Novis, Governor of HMP Leicester speaking at the Applying Shakespeare Symposium convened by the author and Robert Shaughnessy at the Shakespeare Institute, University of Birmingham 9th March 2018. Novis was speaking about the range of activities he has enabled at HMP Leicester – from gospel choirs, big bands and football projects to a 2018 initiative entitled 'Space is the Place' as different creative projects appeal to different people and by having a range of them the prison is able to engage more men in meaningful activity and often to improve their social and educational skills in a non-traditional way.

Chapter 7
Mind the Gap
Working across Lines of Difference in Carceral Shakespeare

Frannie Shepherd-Bates and Kate Powers

Introduction

We, Frannie Shepherd-Bates and Kate Powers, have, between us, more than twenty-five years' experience working as teaching artists, facilitators and directors behind prison walls. While each of us has worked in both men's and women's facilities, Shepherd-Bates has extensive experience working in Michigan's only prison for women, Huron Valley Correctional Facility, while Powers has extensive experience working in men's maximum-security environments in both New York and Minnesota. We stand on the shoulders of the teaching artists, facilitators, scholars and, most importantly, the incarcerated folx who have come before us. We are indebted to them for the discoveries they have made, the vulnerabilities they have chosen to share and the expertise with which they have thoughtfully written

Notes for this section begin on page 128.

about various aspects of performing arts in carceral spaces. In this chapter, we look at the value of the work for participants and explore a gap in the existing literature around the differences in working with men and women. What is the relationship between the ways in which men and women experience trauma and the ways in which they are socialised to cope? How does that impact the structure and value of prison theatre programmes for participants, as well as the ways in which they choose to participate?

Powers's Experience

Kate Powers has facilitated workshops in acting, directing, text analysis, Shakespeare and clown since she began making theatre with incarcerated men in January 2009, as a volunteer facilitator with Rehabilitation Through the Arts (RTA) at Sing Sing Correctional Facility, a maximum-security facility just north of New York City. RTA was founded at Sing Sing in 1996 by Katherine Vockins and the men who comprised the first theatre workshop. The organisation now offers workshops in theatre, dance, creative writing and visual arts in addition to staging full productions for people who are incarcerated in six different facilities, at both maximum and medium levels of security, and is poised to expand into two additional facilities by 2024.

After working as a facilitator and director with RTA for seven years, Powers founded the Redeeming Time Project (RTP) in 2016 with an ensemble of men who were incarcerated at the Minnesota Correctional Facility at Moose Lake. At RTP, Powers built a programme that, like RTA and so many of our sibling programmes, invites participants into a circle that is predicated on a restorative justice-inflected approach.

Shepherd-Bates's Experience

Frannie Shepherd-Bates founded Shakespeare in Prison (SIP) in 2012 under the auspices of Magenta Giraffe Theatre Company, of which she was artistic director; the programme became part of Detroit Public Theatre in 2015. Since its founding, SIP has worked with nearly three hundred incarcerated people at Women's Huron Valley Correctional Facility (Michigan's only prison for women), a minimum-security men's prison and several residential youth facilities. SIP's flagship model was developed by the women's ensemble, beginning in 2012; SIP's men's ensemble, which ran for two years, made several adaptations (such as the use of two different editions of each play), which, when shared by facilitators with the women's ensemble, were adopted by them and made a permanent feature of the flagship model. A traditional in-person season of SIP lasts approximately forty weeks; the program has also had great success with fourteen-week workshops and a two-week intensive course.

In 2018, SIP expanded its work through Shakespeare Reclaimed, a post-release programme for alumni who have left prison. SIP works with alumni on various projects, the most prominent of which is the forthcoming *Richard III in Prison: A Critical Edition*, the first critical edition of a Shakespeare play created by incarcerated and formerly incarcerated people. The book, for which SIP is currently in the process of identifying a publisher, builds on the rich legacy of annotated Shakespeare texts and explicitly centres the experiences and words of marginalised people without exoticising or exploiting them.

The Value of the Work

Many of our colleagues, including Ashley Lucas, Rob Pensalfini, Jonathan Shailor and Curt Tofteland, have written about the value of working with theatre (and Shakespeare specifically) behind prison walls, and we invite readers to explore their vital, substantial contributions to the field. In this section, we will give a broad overview of the work's value, which we see as being largely the same for incarcerated men and women, and focus on our own observations as they relate to what our programmes have in common and to what we perceive as a gap in the literature exploring gender-specific differences.

Jonathan Shailor has observed that making theatre together facilitates the creation of connections and community, a sanctuary space within the rigidity of the prison environment as well as a crucible for self-transformation.[1] Building upon Shailor's work (among many others), SIP conducted a case study of its 2016–17 season with the women's ensemble, which found that the programme's core outcome was the positive development of each participant's narrative identity—how they interpret their past, define their present and envision their future—through a combination of theatrical and operational processes. In the spring and summer of 2020, SIP staff completed a follow-up report that evaluates the long-term results of SIP involvement. The report is centred around formal interviews with eleven formerly incarcerated alumnae that focused on a series of questions about their narrative identities in terms of their past, present and future selves. This report found that the SIP experience has three long-lasting effects on its participants: enhanced self-efficacy, more fully developed empathy for oneself and others, and a positive sense of community. The original case study was conducted prior to SIP having a men's ensemble; to be consistent, follow-up interviews were conducted only with female alumni, but SIP staff have observed that the findings seem to hold true for SIP's male participants. SIP's self-study thus far has been focused on overall outcomes and has not yet defined, or even truly explored, where the work and outcomes may differ between men's and women's ensembles; this became of interest after the original case study was complete and facilitators' work with the men's ensemble led to the questions posed in this chapter.

Participants in prison theatre programmes learn to work together as a team, resolve problems constructively and peacefully, express emotions, take the risk of vulnerability, practise empathy and compassion, set goals, understand themselves and others more deeply and achieve something that can make them and their families proud; they also learn what it means to give back to and become a responsible member of the community. In post-workshop evaluations, participants have shared what was most valuable to them: 'Humility. You learn to place your attention on others with you, before you and after you. Never looking at your own interests alone but to the interests of the group and our shared task'; 'Risk-taking, hard work, confidence, openness to new ideas: so many other lessons are being learned and I didn't even realise it at the time'; and 'Being able to perform in front of friends and family; it gave me something to be proud of (as well as my family)'. Another participant appreciated, upon reflection, the value and the difficulty of being in relationship with other ensemble members: 'Understanding that I had to be empathetic and supportive as my scene partner was battling through his struggle while still making sure I did my part in the scene. It really challenged me to be my better self.'

The arts do not depend upon an academic education or any prerequisites; theatre meets people where they are. Theatre is experiential. There is rarely one correct answer. Working with Shakespeare's text, specifically, can challenge one's assumptions, ask one to sit with polysemy, and expand one's world view; as Rob Pensalfini observes, the deepest of truths are embedded in these plays: 'the capacity to sustain complexity is a quality that is essential for humans to act as effective free agents in an increasingly complex world.'[2]

Through rehearsal room disagreements about the interpretation of a scene, or a line, one can learn to tolerate not just different points of view but ambiguity itself, which can be difficult in the rigidly defined prison atmosphere. RTP ensemble members have written about the value of 'gaining new perspectives' and 'becoming a better communicator'. This newly acquired tolerance and wider understanding of human behaviour helps cultivate patience and perspective; another ensemble member reflected, 'It constructively demands thoughts and actions, crosses racial barriers and breaks down stereotypes.' Heightened language – because of its complexity and because, for both good and ill, Shakespeare occupies an exalted status in our culture – helps us to remember that we are part of the wider circle of humanity. Pensalfini notes that there is no 'whatever' in Shakespeare; 'characters care deeply about their world and articulate their thoughts, feelings, and experiences in precise, passionate language.'[3] An SIP participant reflected,

> It's so easy and it's so natural to dig into yourself when you get into Shakespeare because there's so many ways you can interpret these characters, and there's so many avenues you can go down, especially when you're working with other people who are also figuring out how many ways they can interpret these characters.

Shakespeare challenges us to think in complex ways, to engage with rhetoric intellectually, emotionally and physically; he also invites us to sit with ambiguity. This is particularly crucial, challenging and liberating in an environment that is designed to dehumanise people and channel them into a system that is rigidly, purposefully black and white (as well as Black and white). Further, because of the rarefied place Shakespeare occupies culturally, for a population that has been systematically told that they are 'monsters', 'animals', 'garbage', 'stupid', 'beyond redemption', taking ownership of Shakespeare's language is often a pathway to renewed self-worth and reconnection with others. The men in the RTP ensemble began their first workshop by understanding the power in Shakespeare's words – 'Man, Shakespeare could bring it!' – but there is so much calcified opinion around Shakespeare as 'cultural church' that there was a very real fear in the room of *getting it wrong*. As they realised that they absolutely had the capacity to harness this power and that it could energise them, they stood taller: 'In here, I am not an offender; I'm a human.'

Participants in prison theatre programmes realise what it is to be seen, heard and accepted for who they are, and not for the mistakes they have made. While this happens initially within the circle, in relationship to other ensemble members and to the facilitators, it also starts to filter into visits with family, into the ways in which ensemble members begin to be perceived as trustees by correctional officers and into how other incarcerated folx start to perceive ensemble members as thought leaders and mentors. One RTP member reported, only six weeks after the first workshop had begun, that his wife noticed a change in his openness with her during their visits: 'What happened to the grumpy old guy?'

Participants learn to read visual cues, to listen and observe, to risk ridicule, to build trust. As one RTA participant said, 'I didn't know what trust was. I had never experienced trust in my whole life. I couldn't look anyone in the eye. Then you people come in here and all you want is to make a play with me.' This speaks to the important role facilitators from the outside play in affirming each participant's humanity – sometimes simply by making eye contact and shaking their hand. An SIP ensemble member shared,

> I completely gave up when I started doing time. I was ready for Russian Roulette. Seriously. Somebody give me a gun, and I'll keep pulling the trigger till I get a bullet ... [But when I performed my first Shakespeare monologue] I felt like for the first time, I spoke about what I felt, and people heard me. I thought, 'I can use this as a way to work through that.'... Everyone gave up on me. But there's one person ... [to Frannie] one person who didn't. Shakespeare has been the true source of my healing.

These kinds of healthy relationships – forged through theatre – provide the foundation for participants to affirm their own humanity, gain empathy for themselves and others and do the hard work of reframing their experiences as they redefine their identities beyond the inmate number they've been assigned.

No matter a given programme's methods or measures of outcomes, prison theatre participants often describe their experience in remarkably similar ways. One RTP ensemble member observed,

> One of the greatest values of the work to me was the power of expression, voice and re-found humanity. Prison is a place that strips away

individualism and expression from the people housed there ... While attending Redeeming Time workshops, I was asked to examine things deep down inside of me that I had long ago put away. This gave me a fuller sense of self, as well as a reclamation of some of the humanity the prison system took away.

An SIP alumna said, 'In Shakespeare, no one is invisible. We all matter – we matter to each other. We're more than our crimes – we're more than our sentences. We're people.'

Common Culture and Practices

RTP and SIP have more in common than not. Both approach the work through a restorative justice lens, framed in the values and practices of Augusto Boal's Theatre of the Oppressed. Restorative justice, which developed in Indigenous communities, perceives crime not as a violation of the law, but as a harm to individuals, relationships and communities. A restorative justice conference or circle creates an opportunity to repair harm, to engage with those one has harmed and to work for transformation in people, relationships and communities.

What this means for our work is that the circle, in each case, is an ensemble, and the ensemble makes the decisions. We are non-hierarchical and fully collaborative; sometimes things move very slowly, but every ensemble member has a say. Within each circle, participants have opportunities to engage with one another and the facilitators as human beings, and to practise empathy. The circle restores some of the individual agency that the institution works to strip away. Many of our respective ensemble members find their footing and reassert their voices as we move at the speed of trust. We welcome and consider others' perspectives in a respectful, collaborative exploration. We celebrate failures when they are born out of real efforts to learn. We believe that human beings are born inherently good. As Judy Dworin has written, 'bad choices are not synchronous with bad people',[4] and a trauma-informed approach to the work of theatre behind prison walls foregrounds the questions 'What happened to you?' and 'Who do you want to be?' rather than 'What's wrong with you?' or 'What did you do?' Jelani Cobb has posed the question 'Whose life do we recognise as valuable?',[5] and we posit that by creating opportunities for incarcerated ensemble members to engage with traumatic experiences through both the critical distance Shakespeare's text offers and the invitation to connect, carceral Shakespeare not only has the potential to restore dignity, but also to repair community both inside the walls and outside. An RTA ensemble member said, 'Shakespeare gave me words for feelings I didn't know I had.'

We acknowledge the importance of decolonising and democratising Shakespeare, and we do this by foregrounding participants' perspectives on the work. Both of our programmes invite participants to take ownership of Shakespeare and the creative process, from interpreting the text to conceptualising the performance. These programmes are, very explicitly, neither classes nor traditional rehearsal processes. We resist anything that enforces the norms – and power dynamics – of a traditional classroom. Process is prioritised over product and personal empowerment over artistry. For example, when an SIP ensemble member struggled with her lines to the point that she considered leaving the program, Shepherd-Bates suggested that she write her own version of her monologue. At the next session, the woman felt much more confident and shared, 'You said you'd rather have me than the lines. That feels really good, because you don't hear that that much. And that makes me want to work harder and learn my lines more.'

RTP and SIP have practices in common that go beyond this philosophical approach or even Shakespeare as a focal point. Both groups begin each session with a check-in to make sure everyone in the room has the opportunity to share what's going on with them, in order to be more fully present for the work – and for all participants to practise listening. It's a way to share or release strong feelings that may otherwise overwhelm the room. SIP check-ins are generally followed, but sometimes preceded, by an exercise in which the ensemble envisions a ring of white light above the circle, lowers it to the ground together and spreads it all over the room; each session is bookended by raising the ring back up. RTP checks out at the end: 'What do you want to reinforce? What will you take away from our work together tonight? What do you want to know more about?' Each person in the circle, incarcerated and free, can express gratitude or reflect on a discovery or a moment of difficulty or mirth. Then the ensemble laughs for forty-five seconds, even if they don't feel like it, right before they part company. While this often starts as forced, social laughter, the sustained laughter and eye contact often cross over into Duchenne laughter – reaching the eyes, filled with genuine joy – releasing dopamine, endorphins and serotonin, and releasing stress. Participants have said, 'The laughing exercise we finish with lets me walk out of the class energised and positive', and 'laughing is great medicine'. Effective and repeatable warm-ups are a tool that ensemble members can take with them out of the programme, out of the facility and back into their lives. Starting each session with the same activity creates a sense of stability and a container for participants, allowing them to build skill and confidence through practice. It also invites ensemble members to take ownership of each exercise and eventually lead it themselves.

Physical warm-ups are significant in each of our programmes. The RTP ensemble warms up their bodies with a Patsy Rodenberg 'second circle' presence exercise,[6] to get grounded and to shake off the day; they move on to a scaffolded set of Linklater-informed vocal exercises.[7] The SIP women's ensemble is sometimes averse to physical warm-ups, preferring to jump right into the work, but most ensemble members enjoy Michael Chekhov's 'Staccato/Legato' exercise (renamed by the group as 'Six Directions'),[8] which requires the use of one's entire body to imagine stretching, reaching or pushing energy out from one's centre infinitely.

Games and improvisational exercises are another shared practice. One of RTP's exercises centres around the 'O for a muse of fire' speech that opens *Henry V*. Groups of two to three participants are given the individual words of each line on large pieces of tagboard, to arrange in whatever order they choose. When the ensemble did this exercise in fall 2017, after a few rounds of exploration and tableaux, they reordered the language as Shakespeare's text survives; for the first time, the men began performing an entire section of Shakespearean text as the prologue, passing from one group to the next, made its way around the room with blossoming confidence. There was a moment of delicious theatrical silence after 'affright the air at Agincourt' (1.0.14) when everyone took in what they had heard. They just told one another a story; the power in the words was vibrating in the air around them. 'Can we do that again?' The men were not afraid now of not 'getting it right'; the words belonged to them. Powers asked, 'What does it mean, taken all together?' After a few runs at it by other men, L. said, almost too quietly to be heard, 'It's like – after all these stories, will Harry live up to the hype?'

Through games, we access joy and play. When we celebrate mistakes in those games – actually applauding and inviting the participant to take a deep, operatic bow – we destigmatise and disaggregate the person from the error. We reinforce that making mistakes is part of how we learn, and not necessarily a reason for shame. These somatic experiences of joy and play start to create a culture apart from the rest of the prison, which slowly opens a gateway to exploring other intense emotions within the shared, liminal space of our workshop, within the prison yet distinct from it.

SIP's approach to games and improvisation changes from season to season in response to each ensemble's unique needs and dynamics. Most ensembles have embraced and focused on performative improv games, but some have preferred to concentrate on exercises from the Theatre of the Oppressed, Michael Chekhov technique or both – particularly in the women's ensemble. The feeling of vulnerability that can come from performance can take months for some women to overcome, due to their extreme discomfort with occupying space with their bodies in front of an 'audience', and focusing on exercises that feel safer helps ensemble members who would otherwise be too overwhelmed stay in the room.

Two years after the COVID-19 pandemic began, RTP ensemble member Matt said,

> Losing prison programming during the pandemic was like having a part of my life ripped away ... I had to completely alter the way I was living my life and passing time in prison. I missed the social interaction as well as the mental and social stimulation I received from all the programmes I was involved in.

Specifically, he talked about the value of the presence exercises for him during the lockdown:

> In RTP especially, I learned many coping mechanisms and practices that helped me through those lonely times. During the pandemic, we were isolated from anyone outside of the facilities – volunteers as well as family and friends could no longer see us. But we still had our incarcerated peers ... Prison programming created a community for us that carried on after the programming was taken away.

Working across Lines of Difference

All three programmes strive to facilitate with as much transparency as the carceral system will allow, while also honouring the boundaries it demands. Both RTP and SIP perceive a significant value in having at least two facilitators in the room at all times, ideally working across some line of difference, whether that is gender, race, ability or sexual orientation. Apart from the multiplicity of perspectives this brings, it enables facilitators to model healthy, platonic relationships with those who are different from ourselves. As a woman working primarily with incarcerated men, Powers has had the opportunity to build strong relationships with the men that are platonic and supportive. In some cases, ensemble members have had little experience of healthy platonic relationships across gender differences.

Powers asked one of the men at Sing Sing several years ago if he thought it was odd that the majority of RTA facilitators were white women; he said he had never really considered it because that was almost universally his experience. Another ensemble member, reflecting on RTA's production of Tracy Letts's play *Superior Donuts*, said that at first, he did not like the play because he didn't believe a white person would ever make a sacrifice for a Black person like that which the character Arthur makes for Franco, 'but then', he said to Powers, 'I realised you do that for me'.[9] We offer this not to excuse the harm that white women as a cohort have caused to Black men in particular, but to illustrate that there are opportunities here for connection, for fresh experiences and perspectives. Reflecting on the racial dynamics of this work is beyond the scope of this chapter, but, like gender, it is informed by how each of us, incarcerated or free, has been socialised, as well as how we then choose to behave with regard to the disinformation and stereotypes we've been taught in our overwhelmingly white supremacist capitalist culture.

RTP ensemble member Matt wrote about the re-socialising benefits of working with facilitators of different genders:

> As a male participant in RTP I felt that I was most comfortable interacting with the male facilitators. Being in a men's prison, I was not used to interacting with women very often, and if I did, they were prison staff or family members. It made the interactions more awkward at first but I became more comfortable as time went on. Programmes like RTP help participants relearn that we are just people. The contrast of different genders is noticeable at first but as everyone becomes familiar with each other these differences fade ... RTP gave me a deeper sense of self, but also a deeper sense of other people. Especially those of a different gender.

RTA ensemble member Tim reinforced the importance of having an opportunity to develop positive social and adaptive capabilities through working with facilitators who identify as women; likewise, SIP women's ensemble members place a great deal of value on working with male facilitators, albeit for reasons stemming from differential traumas and socialisation.

Initially, the SIP women's ensemble's decision to bring in its first male facilitator was based on their desire for a different perspective on the material, but the value of having a sensitive, compassionate man in the room turned out to be far greater. Many ensemble members had survived trauma at the hands of men and had grown to distrust all men. But, as one woman tearfully reflected during a season wrap-up:

> Guys are nice. They're not all sleazeballs ... I used to think, am I ever going to be able to look at men and not see something sick inside of them? But [facilitator] Kyle's just a normal guy, and it gives me hope for my future. If I hadn't had you as a male around me, I wouldn't have been able to grow like I have, for my life on the outside. I'm gonna be normal again, and it's gonna be okay.

People on the outside often assume that a women's ensemble would baulk at how many characters in Shakespeare's canon are male But SIP's female participants tend not to see the point of changing a character's gender, and many of them enjoy the feelings of power and confidence they experience while playing men – occupying bodies that trauma and socialisation have taught them are more powerful than theirs – no matter the play or character. One woman said, 'The fact that we had an all-female cast reassured me that women are capable of doing just about anything they put their minds to, as well as me'. The first time an ensemble member changed their character's gender was during SIP's eighth season, when the woman who played the Captain in *Twelfth Night* proposed making her character female only because 'we haven't done it yet ... and I want the outfit to be super cute'. The ensemble agreed, and the Captain's costume ended up being a large, floppy 'pirate hat' that was black with lace and red ribbons, a red lace-up vest over a white sleeveless shirt, and black pants with boots.

The Divergence

Approximately 71 per cent of correctional officers in the United States are men; just shy of 90 per cent of the humans we incarcerate are men. For comparison, based on UK Ministry of Justice figures, women account for 50 per cent of HMPPS staff as of 31 March 2021, although they are more heavily represented in probation staff than prison staff. Men are never more than 45 per cent of the correctional officers at public sector prisons for women in the UK, and frequently comprise closer to 30 per cent of correctional staff.[10] Women are more likely to be incarcerated for non-violent crimes than men. Their rates of substance abuse are slightly higher. But American prisons have largely been designed with men in mind, and women's prisons have not been modified or designed to account for their different needs. Prison clothing was made to fit male bodies, as Keri Blakinger writes in the *Washington Post*, and policies, processes and punishments have been built to 'control male social structures and male violence'.[11] Because women comprise a significantly smaller portion of the incarcerated population, they are subject to what Blakinger identifies as an 'economy of scale', meaning that incarcerated women often have access to far fewer educational and job training programmes than do their male counterparts. Andrew Coyle has observed that 'There is a recurring tendency that any special provision for women prisoners will be something that is added on to the standard provision for men'.[12] Male officers often oversee incarcerated women in their housing units – although this is not the case in Michigan, where a 1996 class action lawsuit on behalf of incarcerated women who were 'subjected to sexual abuse, sexual harassment, privacy violations by male [prison] staff ... and/or retaliation for reporting such abuse while incarcerated in a Michigan Department of Corrections (MDOC) facility' resulted in a $100 million settlement and the removal of male officers 'from areas where they could view women while they were nude or partially clothed'. In many states, women have to purchase feminine hygiene products at the commissary; if they do not have money in their accounts, they have to improvise when they get their period. Even where there is a state law stipulating access to feminine hygiene products, individual wardens and superintendents may require incarcerated women to ask for products from correctional officers, which can be humiliating.

According to Elizabeth Swavola et al., 86 per cent of incarcerated women in the United States have experienced sexual violence in their lives, 77 per cent report intimate partner violence and 60 per cent have survived caregiver violence; 79 per cent of incarcerated women are also mothers who have been separated from their children.[13]

Men are, of course, just as likely to be separated from their children as are women, but the mothers of those children are still caring for them; incarcerated women are often single mothers, so, to paraphrase US Attorney General Loretta Lynch, the whole family is incarcerated, or disrupted, to a greater extent.[14] When the mother is incarcerated, children may be cared for by another family member, but are at greater risk of moving into the foster care system. This could mean a longer, or even a permanent, separation from one's children post-release. Under the federal Adoption and Safe Families Act (ASFA), whenever a child has lived in foster care for fifteen of the most recent twenty-two months, the state is required to file a petition to terminate parental rights. According to the US Sentencing Commission, the median minimum sentence for a female offender in the federal prison system is twenty-nine months;[15] ASFA makes no exception for incarcerated parents. Furthermore, women's prisons are rarely family-friendly in the design of housing units, visiting areas, playgrounds or, indeed, in terms of policy vis-à-vis visits with children or training for correctional officers who may encounter children on a visit.

While exposure to trauma is also prevalent among men who are incarcerated in the US, Nancy Wolff et al. have reported that, before age 18, physical abuse is more likely than sexual abuse for boys, while the two varieties of abuse occur at equal rates for girls.[16] Wolff et al. also estimated 'sexual inmate-on-inmate victimization rates over a 6-month period at 3.2% for female inmates and 1.5% for male inmates. The risk of victimization doubled for female inmates who experienced sexual abuse prior to age 18.'[17] Wolff and her colleagues further found that, while incarcerated, men were significantly more likely to experience physical violence, whether inmate-on-inmate or staff-on-inmate, whereas sexual victimisation is more common for women who are incarcerated, and is more likely to be perpetrated by another incarcerated individual than a member of correctional staff: '7% of males (18% of those reporting any victimisation) and 11% of females (31% of those reporting any victimisation) report experiencing both forms of victimisation by other inmates, staff, or both inmates and staff over a 6-month period.'[18] Wolff and her colleagues identify a strong concordance between 'childhood and adult victimisation', as well as 'gender patterns in the experiences of and reactions to victimisation over the life cycle'. According to the US Bureau of Justice Statistics, more than half of incarcerated women also note an ongoing medical issue, in comparison with only 35 per cent of incarcerated men.[19]

As Stephen Porges has observed, this can mean that all prison theatre participants, across genders, are living with a heightened sense of neuroception, perceiving danger in processes that may read like standard operating procedure to someone who has not experienced assault or other violence. This can manifest in flat facial affect, a loss of complex language (because the traumatised brain has redirected its focus away from Broca's area, which is linked to speech), decreases in relational ability and even immobilisation behaviours when the perception of danger is at its greatest.[20] Swavola et al. report 'that gender-responsive factors including trauma, mental illness, substance abuse, relationship problems, and parental stress either occur with greater frequency among women than men or affect women in unique personal and social ways'.[21] The authors point out that 'searches, restraints, and use of solitary confinement' can reactivate trauma.

While each American state and the federal government have their own correctional systems, with idiosyncratic differences, the binary gender divide is common to them all, so we are framing the discussion in terms of women's facilities and men's facilities. Powers has worked with trans men who were incarcerated in women's facilities and with trans women in men's facilities. Overwhelmingly, in the US, trans folx are not housed in facilities that match their gender identity, which presents yet another set of challenges for participants and facilitators to negotiate. In general terms, both of our ensembles, regardless of gender, are welcoming to non-binary and trans participants; this is true despite differences in the levels of accommodation or tolerance specific facilities and correctional staffs make for gender non-conforming people.

The types of trauma and the relational expression appear to be different between our two ensembles. We are curious about the relationship between the aforementioned data and the women's frequent reluctance to move and be fully physically present, in contrast with the anxiety surrounding emotional vulnerability among the men. The women have far less trouble connecting emotionally with scene partners, perhaps because of emotional bonds created in the physical stillness of the reading and discussion part of the process, while the men generally enjoy physical performance but take more time to connect emotionally with each other onstage. We acknowledge, and strive to adjust our practices to, the needs of our ensembles, but neither we nor our co-facilitators are therapists. In the following sections, Powers will use examples from several workshops to illustrate trauma-specific challenges and solutions she has observed in her work with incarcerated men; Shepherd-Bates will focus on one season that highlights her observations that seem specific to women.

There is a great deal of 'fronting' inside men's maximum security spaces, what Ben Crewe and colleagues refer to, variously, as working to 'maintain an appearance of cool indifference', performing 'masculine bravado' and striving 'to develop a persona which saves [one] from exploitation'.[22] Fronting – in effect, performing gender – can manifest in how a man carries himself, how much time he spends working out in the yard and in vocal changes that convey a 'don't mess with me' signal to his peers. This performance of a more masculine self, this occlusion of deep feeling, is a survival strategy for many incarcerated men; showing deep emotion can, in an environment of supercharged masculinity, suggest that one is weak, a potential target. In exploring the scaffolded range of exercises that Linklater delineates in *Freeing the Natural Voice*, men in the RTA and RTP ensembles have, over time, rediscovered their voices quite literally: accessing a pitch, timbre and tone that they have concealed from themselves for years. Powers has observed men bursting into joyful laughter and also into tears when they first hear this sound again. Re-accessing that which has been closed off often becomes a first step towards being able to explore openness and vulnerability when one wants to, such as in rehearsal or during a visit.

From their very first workshop together, the men in the RTP ensemble were consistently willing to throw themselves into any physical exploration or activity that interrogated status, power relationships, how a character might carry himself, ways of moving through space and how changes in physicality could open up understanding of a character or an embedded stage direction. They were initially uncomfortable, however, holding eye contact with a scene partner. Steady eye contact can be an invitation to reveal oneself; it can be perceived as a challenge. Further, it can intensify feelings of shame. In the carceral environment, where openness can equate with weakness, and where 'the excessive display of emotion is to be avoided at all costs',[23] sustained eye contact can be multiply fraught.

In early sessions, facilitators had to pivot because some exercises were too uncomfortable for the ensemble as a cohort. During one activity that invited ensemble members to move about the space and then come to stillness across from a partner, the majority of the men, who had been engaged while exploring other prompts, exhibited tension in the jaw or shoulders and shifted from foot to foot. There was nervous laughter and a fair amount of crosstalk. The men would not directly say that they were uncomfortable; they would try to muscle through. Powers perceived that they did not want to let her down, nor did they want to admit to what they judged to be a weakness. RTP facilitators pivoted from these kinds of high-focus exercises to lower-focus activities, where ensemble members could explore their emotional responses simultaneously but independently. With the lower level of scrutiny, knowing that every ensemble member was doing his own work, participants were more willing to explore and, to borrow Curt Tofteland's phrase, to walk towards what scared them.[24]

Over the course of several weeks, the men began to share what they discovered as the ensemble debriefed an exercise or activity. As participants became more comfortable making eye contact, as the RTP ensemble developed their circle of trust, facilitators worked to scaffold exercises so that the vulnerability 'ask' increased gently but perceptibly over the course of several weeks. In rehearsing a scene that called for a character to collapse with grief, an incarcerated actor was uncomfortable taking this risk and asked Powers to demonstrate what that might look like. While she might not demonstrate an acting choice like this with professional actors, she judged that modelling this combination of physical and emotional vulnerability might 'give permission' or relieve some anxiety about perceived weakness for the ensemble. Late in that first sixteen-week workshop, as they saw how emotional engagement made scene-work more exciting to watch, the men were drawing connections among exercises and games from the first week through the first performance, encouraging one another to 'tell it like it is, man', and demonstrating by example a willingness to be more emotionally available.

Where men tend to feel less vulnerable in occupying physical space than in their emotional lives, the opposite is generally true with SIP women's ensemble members. Women who join SIP are often 'shut down' as a result of the many types of trauma outlined above; they are often reluctant to get on their feet to perform Shakespeare or participate in improv exercises. The less space the women take up, the safer they feel. They need a great deal of support from the ensemble and facilitators in order to push themselves out of their 'comfort zone', so the women's ensemble focuses more on breaking through barriers to physicality than on the emotional 'dam-breaking' Shepherd-Bates observed in her two years' work with men. SIP's *Twelfth Night* season (2018–19) provides clear illustrations not only of this gender-specific, trauma-related challenge, but of the factors that enabled the SIP women's ensemble to overcome it: leadership and 'permission' from fellow ensemble members; theatre expertise, modelling and support from a female facilitator; and working across lines of difference with male facilitators around whom they could feel safe.

Towards the end of each SIP season, the ensemble chooses the next season's play. In the spring of 2018, the group selected *Twelfth Night*, specifically because they wanted to work on something light and fun. By that fall, when the *Twelfth Night* season began, several core ensemble members, who had always energetically thrown themselves into analysis, performance and encouraging newbies to step out of their 'comfort zone' as soon as they felt ready, had been paroled. This created a leadership vacuum that facilitators expected would quickly and organically be filled, but nearly all new members were very uncomfortable doing anything that required physical commitment, and it was often a challenge to get people even to speak or read aloud. The ensemble struggled to find points in the text for lively discussion when reading while seated, and with only a few participants willing to read on their feet, let alone dip their toes into performance, the group became bogged down by a feeling of inertia.

One of SIP's core values is that ensemble members are 'nudged' out of their comfort zone, but never 'pushed' to do Shakespeare or anything else; it is understood that it often takes time to build confidence and trust, and the priority is always to maintain a space that is safe for all. Facilitators did not know how to address this new dynamic within SIP's non-hierarchical model, so, eight weeks into this forty-week season, Shepherd-Bates advised the ensemble that they would need to collaborate to solve the problem or the process would become increasingly frustrating, and perhaps fall apart entirely.

S., who had been in the group for several years and was extremely uncomfortable occupying physical space, challenged herself and the group to do exactly that, even though it scared them. This unprecedented leadership from someone who was clearly pushing herself so far out of her 'comfort zone' inspired the ensemble to push themselves, and each other, in kind, and literally, physically rise to the occasion. This not only created a more active and energetic ethos, it enhanced the safe space they'd already created.

This, in turn, helped B., a new member who was extremely withdrawn and fearful of physical contact, feel comfortable enough to open up to the group: 'I get scared to [perform] because I don't know what anyone's gonna do. But I think if no one touches me, I might be able to do it.' All agreed to keep their distance and thanked B. for her candour. This expression of her own vulnerability made B., unintentionally, another leader and inspired J., a long-time member, to provide strong encouragement (and nudging) that enabled B. to push herself ever further out of her comfort zone – including taking on multiple lead roles in the play. B.'s consistent courage inspired S. to become increasingly active as a leader, specifically in her compassionate scene-work with women who were hesitant about 'doing Shakespeare wrong'. This, in turn, inspired J., and the two developed a rapport as they guided and encouraged not only B., but all hesitant ensemble members to 'dive in' to the process and performance. This symbiotic leadership from incarcerated ensemble members was the first factor that enabled the ensemble to collectively overcome trauma-related fears and challenges. Everyone felt safe and supported within the circle.

The second factor in the season's success was Shepherd-Bates's ability to lead theatrical exercises that supported the group's need to gain comfort in their bodies without reactivating past trauma. 'Mirrors' exercises from the Theatre of the Oppressed[25] provided a major turning point. These partner exercises require concentration, eye contact and vulnerability as the 'subject' leads the 'image' through a series of physical movements that must be copied as exactly as possible, and partners take turns being either 'subject' or 'image'. Importantly, the mirror exercises Shepherd-Bates chose did not require physical contact, but movement in and of itself was challenging for many women, especially expansive movements and poses. Their partners did not try to force them to do what they were clearly uncomfortable with; they adapted so they could stay together. 'I didn't know, like, how your body could look happy or whatever', one woman reflected. 'I feel like you can only really express that with your face.' Shepherd-Bates pointed out that this disconnection from their bodies comes from the way women are socialised: *not to take up space*. 'I *can't* just express joy with my face', Shepherd-Bates said. 'I *need* my whole body. I need to do something like *this*!' She demonstrated a few large gestures and a happy dance. 'It's *hard* to go that big, isn't it? Especially if you've experienced trauma. Because it makes us vulnerable.'

The ensemble's commedia dell'arte-inflected concept for *Twelfth Night* required them to 'go big', and they asked Shepherd-Bates to become more directly involved as a performer than had been SIP's practice since its founding. 'For some reason', one woman said, 'when you're up there with us, it gives off the confidence to do what we want to do'. Another participant added, 'That energy, it just opened me up!' Shepherd-Bates was cast as a *Zanni* – a silly clown with no lines – and endeavoured to boost the group's energy with total physical commitment to 'shtick' like tango dancing with an inflatable palm tree. This adjustment was similar to the modelling Powers described earlier, but made for entirely different reasons: it wasn't emotional vulnerability that the women needed modelled, but physical ease and confidence. The ensemble also asked Shepherd-Bates to lead more in staging challenging scenes; this gave them a better understanding of the material from which to build their staging and performances.

The third crucial factor was the consistent presence of, and support from, a male facilitator – at this time, Matthew Van Meter, SIP's then assistant director – who listened to and respected the women, validated their feelings and affirmed their humanity. MDOC policy prohibited physical contact, for all facilities, regardless of gender, which released the women from any fear they had about being touched. During the season wrap-up, one woman shared that Matthew was 'the only man I've ever been able to trust. I can be near you, and I don't freak out. I feel safe ... I've never, ever had that before. You're what a man should be.'

Conclusion

We appreciate this opportunity to explore these differences that we have observed, but could not initially codify or name, between our work with incarcerated men and women. We hear remarkably similar reports from our respective ensembles – and, indeed, from the circles in which many of our colleagues stand – about the humanising value of prison theatre. Our work as practitioners standing in solidarity with incarcerated ensembles has demonstrated that men and women in carceral Shakespeare programmes need different trauma-responsive practices because, first of all, their traumas are different, and, secondly, they have largely been socialised to respond in different ways. In our respective circles, these practices often take the form of multiple points of entry that diverge along gender lines: for the women, a focus on gaining comfort in their bodies and taking up physical space is called for, whereas the men require more scaffolded focus on accessing and taking the risk of expressing their emotional lives. Programming for all genders needs to create a space apart from the authoritative constraints of the wider facility. For the men, this includes extending the invitation in as many ways as possible to stop performing masculinity, and to be fully present as themselves, to take the risk of accessing what the larger prison environment demands that they contain. It's critically important, too, to ensure that, in closing out a workshop session, men have the space to 'close the shutters' on the vulnerability and prepare to re-enter the constrained public space of the facility. For the women, the 'space apart' must be one where they feel safe and supported in venturing outside the emotionally vulnerable, 'broken' place that feels most comfortable and into the power of their own bodies in movement and the occupation of physical space.

We are not social scientists, nor are we trauma experts, although our work is trauma-informed. The absence of gender-specific literature about prison theatre has presented challenges to each of us when we have had the opportunity to work with the population where we had less experience. In order to adapt to the needs of each community, prison theatre practitioners need to better understand experiences and traumas unique to every gender in order to best bridge that divide and best support each ensemble and each individual within each circle. Our experiences are anecdotal, and our observations are qualitative rather than quantitative. While we are not able to unpick the complex carceral tapestry of socialisation, violence and trauma, we both look forward to further study and to partnerships with trauma experts, therapists and sociologists to refine the ways in which we deliver programming that is ever-more attuned to the specific needs of each of these populations.

Frannie Shepherd-Bates is a prison theatre practitioner, director, educator and grant writer. She is the founder and director of Shakespeare in Prison, Detroit Public Theatre's signature community program, which uses Shakespeare's works as a means of empowerment and identity development for incarcerated and formerly incarcerated people. Frannie has directed many plays for south-east Michigan's professional theatres; she has also taught for and directed educational theatre programs for youth, including playwriting and Shakespeare performance. She has been featured numerous times in local, national and international media, including an episode of the Folger Shakespeare Library's 'Shakespeare Unlimited' podcast. She holds a Bachelor of Fine Arts in Acting from Wayne State University.

Kate Powers has directed extensively off-Broadway and regionally, including Steven Dietz's *Becky's New Car* at Theatre Aspen with Sandy Duncan, and Charlotte Jones's *Humble Boy* for the National Theatre's UK National Tour with Hayley Mills. She is founding Artistic Director of the Redeeming Time Project, which uses Shakespeare to effect positive change for the incarcerated and the formerly incarcerated. She has been a facilitator with Rehabilitation through the Arts (www.rta-arts.org, accessed 23 January 2023) at Sing Sing Correctional Facility since 2009. Kate has taught at the Juilliard School, the Conservatory of Theatre at SUNY Purchase, and Carleton College; she is currently visiting faculty at the University of Idaho's Distance MFA Program. A Drama League Directing Fellow and a Fulbright Scholar in Shakespeare, Kate earned her MA with Distinction at the Shakespeare Institute in Stratford-upon-Avon she recently earned her MFA in Directing, with an emphasis on social justice and liberatory pedagogy, from the University of Idaho. She is keenly interested in working to build a more humane, inclusive and anti-racist American theatre.

Notes

1. Jonathan Shailor, *Performing New Lives: Prison Theatre* (London: Jessica Kingsley, 2013).
2. Rob Pensalfini, *Prison Shakespeare: For These Deep Shames and Great Indignities* (New York: Palgrave, 2016), 200.

3. Ibid., 203.
4. Quoted in Shailor, *Performing New Lives*, 88.
5. Quoted in *13th*, dir. Ava DuVernay (USA: Netflix, 2016).
6. Patsy Rodenburg, *Presence* (London: Michael Joseph, 2007), 51–55.
7. Kristin Linklater, *Freeing the Natural Voice* (Hollywood, CA: Drama, 2006).
8. Lenard Petit, *The Michael Chekhov Handbook: For the Actor* (New York: Routledge, 2010), 38–40.
9. The play focuses on the cross-generational, cross-racial relationship between Arthur, a despondent, ageing, white radical, and his enthusiastic but troubled young African American assistant, Franco. Arthur ultimately upends his life in order to help Franco resolve a threat.
10. Ministry of Justice FOIA (November 2013), Male:female staffing ratio of prison officers in women's prisons.
11. Keri Blakinger, 'Can We Build a Better Women's Prison?', *Washington Post*, 28 October 2019.
12. Andrew Coyle, 'Foreword', in Diane C. Hatton and Anastasia A. Fisher (eds), *Women Prisoners and Health Justice* (Oxford: Radcliffe, 2009), vii–ix.
13. Elizabeth Swavola, Kristi Riley and Ram Subramanian, *Overlooked: Women and Jails in an Era of Reform* (New York: Vera Institute of Justice, August 2016).
14. Office of the Attorney General (30 March 2016), 'Attorney General Loretta E. Lynch Delivers Remarks at the White House Women and the Criminal Justice System Convening', https://perma.cc/2KNR-VSZU (accessed 23 January 2023).
15. United States Sentencing Commission (2018), 'Quick Facts on Women in the Federal Offender Population', https://www.ussc.gov.
16. Nancy Wolff, Jing Shi and Jane Siegel, 'Patterns of Victimization among Male and Female Inmates: Evidence of an Enduring Legacy', *Violence and Victims* 24(4) (2009), 469–84.
17. Nancy Wolff, Cynthia Blitz, Jing Shi, Ronet Bachman and Jane Siegel, 'Sexual Violence Inside Prisons: Rates of Victimization', *Journal of Urban Health* 83(5) (2006), 835–48.
18. Wolff et al., 'Patterns'.
19. Laura M. Maruschak, 'Medical Problems of Jail Inmates', *U.S. Department of Justice, Office of Justice Programs, Bureau of Justice Statistics* (Washington, DC), 2 (2006).
20. Stephen Porges, *The Pocket Guide to the Polyvagal Theory: The Transformative Power of Feeling Safe* (New York: W. W. Norton, 2017), 62–72.
21. Swavola, Elizabeth at al. Overloooked: Women and Jails in an Era of Reform, *Vera Institute of Justice*. (August 2016), 14, https://www.vera.org/downloads/publications/overlooked-women-and-jails-report-updated.pdf.
22. Ben Crewe, Jason Warr, Peter Bennett and Alan Smith, 'The Emotional Geography of Prison Life', *Theoretical Criminology* 18(1) (2014), here 56, 57, 61.
23. Gresham M. Sykes, *The Society of Captives* (Princeton, NJ: Princeton University Press, 1958), quoted in Crewe et al., 'Emotional Geography', 58.
24. Shared with Powers in conversation on multiple occasions.
25. Augusto Boal, *Games for Actors and Non-Actors*, 2nd edn (New York: Routledge, 2002), 129–36.

Chapter 8
Signing Shakespeare

Tracy Irish and Abigail Rokison-Woodall

'Signing Shakespeare' began life in 2018 as a small-scale staff research project funded through an ongoing collaboration agreement between the Royal Shakespeare Company and the University of Birmingham. It began with three key questions:

- In what ways can the deaf learner access the language-rich, prosodic world of Shakespeare?
- What, if any, are the benefits to the social and cognitive development of deaf learners offered through working with Shakespeare?
- What benefits can sign language bring to Shakespeare, both for deaf and hearing audiences?

Through research, trial workshops and consultation with deaf practitioners and students and teachers of the deaf,[1] we started to explore these questions. Alongside this, we began to build on our findings and create a scheme of work aimed at deaf learners aged ten to sixteen on one of the most commonly studied texts: *Macbeth*. This resource, now available to access for free on the Royal Shakespeare

Notes for this section begin on page 145.

Company (RSC) website,[2] provides a practical response to our three enquiry questions. The six aims for the resource are: to create enjoyment and understanding of Shakespeare's text; to develop pro-social, collaborative skills; to support social and emotional development; to build understanding of key literary terms; to offer role models for deaf young people; and to celebrate the expressive richness of sign language.[3] The activities focus on visual and active learning, exploring not just the story of *Macbeth* but also the characters, relationships, themes, imagery, rhythms and literary devices of the play. Resources include a series of short filmed scenes performed by deaf actors, along with a package of collaborative activities and writing tasks that support students to develop understanding of the different perspectives and layers within the text.

Although primarily designed to support deaf young people in their study and enjoyment of Shakespeare in response to our first two questions, we hope that Signing Shakespeare also supports our own affirmative response to the third question – that sign language can, indeed, bring significant benefits to both deaf and hearing audiences, due to its inherently expressive, creative and interpretative nature. We hope the resources, particularly the films, make a contribution to celebrating and promoting that value. In this chapter we outline our key findings and the process we engaged in that resulted in the creation of Signing Shakespeare.

Gestures and signs are a natural part of how humans communicate and the use of sign language as a mode of communication for deaf people has undoubtedly been with us throughout human history. The first official record of signing at a ceremony in the UK is from Shakespeare's lifetime, in 1575 in Leicester, when one Thomas Tilsey signed his wedding vows.[4] Sign languages have developed over the centuries in the same ways as any other living language, with new vocabulary and syntax evolving dynamically within commonly accepted standards, passed down through generations. Sign languages are now academically and formally accepted in many parts of the world to be as rich and expressive as spoken languages and are known to follow similar processing routes in the brain.[5] Most deaf people in the UK, however, acquire British Sign Language (BSL) as a second language. The majority of deaf children, around 90 per cent, are born to hearing parents, very few of whom already have knowledge of deafness or skills in signing, and this creates barriers to communication in the home that can lead to disadvantage in personal, social, emotional, physical and academic development.[6]

In 2021, the National Deaf Children's Society reported that in the UK, 78 per cent of deaf children were in mainstream schools, with a further 20 per cent in special schools or special units within schools and only 2 per cent in special schools for the deaf. In those educational settings, 88 per cent of deaf children mainly used spoken language, 7 per cent used spoken language together with signs, 2 per cent used British or Irish Sign Language and 3 per cent used another combination.[7] Noting that BSL is still a minority language among people who are deaf, deaf researcher Robert Adams argues that an agenda of inclusivity that actively prefers to keep children in the mainstream has effectively led to exclusivity. Since most deaf young people do not learn BSL as their first language from parents and carers, their opportunities to learn and interact with sign language are limited, which can exclude them from the rich fluency of signing.[8]

Thomas Braidwood set up the first school for the deaf in Edinburgh in 1760 using what we might now see as the forerunner of Total Communication (TC), a common approach to deaf education in the UK. Carrying on his legacy, Braidwood Trust School for the Deaf in Birmingham defines TC as 'a philosophy of educating deaf learners that incorporates all means of communication; formal signs, natural gestures, fingerspelling, body language, listening, lipreading and speech'.[9] Schools and special units for the deaf aim to provide a language-rich environment for their pupils, with most offering opportunities to develop skills in BSL and often using Sign Supported English (SSE). SSE is not a language as BSL is, with its own vocabulary, syntax and grammar, but a means of communicating that adapts BSL signs for use in spoken English word order. While the BSL Act of 2022 made BSL an official language and paves the way for further developments (such as a GCSE in BSL) students in mainstream schools may have few opportunities to develop their signing skills.

The current education of deaf young people in the UK and across the world still lies in the shadow of the Second International Congress on Education of the Deaf held in Milan in 1880 (the Milan Conference). At this conference, a group of influential hearing educators interrupted the development of deaf education by asserting 'the incontestable superiority of articulation over signs'. This led to a ban on the use of sign language in schools and to hearing, rather than deaf, adults becoming responsible for the learning and communication skills of deaf young people in the classroom. In 2010, the Twenty-First International Congress formally apologised for this damaging move, but 'oralism', the concept that young people should learn through speech in order to become better integrated into society, dominated deaf education in the twentieth century.[10]

There are around fifty-two thousand deaf children in the UK.[11] The majority are required to study the National Curriculum, with Shakespeare as a compulsory element of that curriculum in England. We wondered if there were ways to support that study using our experience of working with Shakespeare in education. As hearing people, we would position ourselves as deaf allies, recognising our lack of experience and expertise of deaf culture but wanting to learn more and to support the learning of deaf young people with the expertise we are able to contribute from our work with Shakespeare. Our project began through Abigail's increased personal interest, having a child diagnosed with auditory neuropathy, a rare form of deafness, and her professional interest, piqued through an encounter with Deafinitely theatre company. She found a research and development (R&D) session with Deafinitley, hosted by the RSC in February 2017, to be a deeply inspiring event that highlighted the creativity and clarity of sign language for appealing both to deaf and hearing audiences. Tracy was invited to join the project to bring her experience of researching and developing theatre-based practice in education – practice that investigates complex texts using activities and principles common to the rehearsal rooms of theatre companies. She was keen to work with deaf artists to learn more about the visual and physical expressive potential of Shakespeare's language.

Throughout the project we have worked closely with Angie Wootten, a colleague in the Disability, Inclusion and Special Needs department of the University of Birmingham with a specialism in deaf education. Angie has long been interested in the value of drama approaches and co-authored a book with Jacqui O'Hanlon in 2007 entitled *Using Drama to Teach Personal, Social and Emotional Skills*.[12] She generously shared her knowledge with us, telling us that there is very little extant research relating to drama and deaf children and, in particular, the teaching of Shakespeare to deaf children. In the 1980s there were glimpses in the literature of practitioners 'having a hunch' that using drama and role play, with its focus on the body, expression and gesture, and perspective-taking, could be a useful tool with deaf children, but little more.[13]

Angie also shared with us key information about deafness and the current understanding of the development of literacy in deaf children. We learned about the wide variety and range of hearing loss indicated by that simple term 'deaf'. Deafness ranges from mild to moderate to severe to profound. A mildly deaf child might struggle to hear a whisper, while a profoundly deaf child might not hear a plane taking off next to them. For many deaf young people, hearing aids or cochlear implants help them to access spoken language and engage with a TC approach. In order to develop age-appropriate spoken language, deaf children need access to hearing aids or cochlear implants early in their life and they need these to be effective for them; they don't work for everyone. In order to develop effective sign language a deaf child needs early exposure to it, which can be challenging, as mentioned above, if they are the first deaf person in their family.

Recent figures show that British deaf students achieve, on average, a grade lower than their hearing peers at GCSE level.[14] It is important to state that deafness in itself is not a learning disability; however, 23 per cent of deaf children have one or more additional learning needs, and for many others, lack of opportunities in acquiring language (either BSL or spoken English) in early development can compound disadvantage. This disadvantage can manifest in the development of literacy skills and complicate the common assumption that if a child cannot hear, they can be given a text to read. With Angie, we also explored the added linguistic challenges that complex texts like Shakespeare bring when meaning is found in the sounds of words through such devices as alliteration, assonance, rhyme, onomatopoeia and puns. We wanted to explore ways in which these aspects of the language, and others, such as metre, personification, metaphor and simile, could be actively explored in order to give deaf children a visceral, physical experience of them.

For the initial project, we set out to examine, through consultations with teachers of the deaf and a week of active, playful investigation with deaf and hearing practitioners, whether the theatre-based approaches used by the RSC in their education work with young people could be of benefit to deaf learners. Increasing evidence from the RSC suggests that such approaches build confidence and resilience, raise aspirations and attainment, and foster a positive attitude towards the study of Shakespeare in young people from many backgrounds and abilities.[15] Adaptations to the exercises are always important, depending on context, and particularly with Special Educational Needs and Disabilities (SEND) groups, but could such methods be adapted or expanded to include and benefit deaf learners using a range of communication methods?

There are key points common across theatre-based practice that build on established good pedagogical principles, and we set out to explore whether these principles still hold true when working with deaf learners. These principles might be summarised as:

- Inviting in a child's prior knowledge, experience and imagination and co-constructively extending their knowledge and skills;
- Asking open questions to encourage dialogic debate and critical thinking;
- Making texts accessible and enjoyable to encourage understanding and promote future engagement;
- Working as a pro-social ensemble to solve the real-world problems of communicating a text to an audience.

Alongside Angie's continuing input and guidance, we consulted with teachers of the deaf from two specialist schools for the deaf. Together with those teachers, we assessed the exercises in the *RSC Toolkit*[16] for challenges and found some obvious issues. Listening exercises, such as asking young people to close their eyes and echo key words as a speech is read aloud, or asking them to stand back to back with their partner to read their lines, are clearly problematic with deaf learners and can make already vulnerable young people feel more vulnerable. Exercises that expect students to move around a space and follow verbal instructions, or repeat lines of text, also clearly need to be modified to allow deaf learners to gain the visual cues they need, whether by lip-reading or watching the signing of an interpreter. Many of the exercises also assume the ability to read a piece of text aloud, individually or in unison, and extra consideration with such exercises needs to be given, as discussed above, to the fact that many deaf learners are disadvantaged in reaching the reading ability of their hearing peers. Many more exercises, however, such as inhabiting characters and settings through freeze-frames and multi-sensory experiences, or finding meaning through physical gestures and rhythm, are as accessible and useful for deaf students as they are for hearing students.

The general principle of 'learning by doing' is a standard pedagogic principle for teachers of the deaf and dovetails neatly with the active drama-focused approaches of theatre-based practice. Its efficacy is explained by the concept of embodied cognition, defined by Lawrence Shapiro and Steven A. Stolz as 'concerned with the interaction of the mind, body and environment in explaining how knowledge is grounded in sensorimotor routines and experiences'.[17] Embodied cognition is a term that captures the increasing scientific understanding that far from being rational minds carried around in unruly emotional bodies, we derive all of our thinking from the patterns and associations laid down in our brains by our emotionally coloured sensory contact with the world around us. All of this sensory, experiential information adds up to the prior knowledge and lived experiences that create each person's unique perspective of how they understand and interact with the world around them.

As highly social animals, we have evolved to be strongly influenced by our contact with other human beings. The active, embodied approaches of theatre-based practice tap into humans' innate embodied cognition, how we learn through the sensory experiences and emotional responses of our whole body and how our comparisons and considerations of the ideas and perspectives of others impact on our personal and social development. Communicating with others allows us to unconsciously but constantly readjust our own personal mental schema of reality. Our understanding is personal because it is filtered through the myriad previous sensory perceptions that have formed our experiences. Language, verbal and non-verbal, is how we share this embodied cognition of the world with others and how others' embodied cognition can affect and readjust our own understanding of the world. Members of the deaf community are often more connected with their bodies and so can teach oral/aural people much about embodied cognition in practice. Shakespeare voice and text doyen Cicely Berry, with an acknowledgement of 'the deaf speaker', calls this 'the physicality of language'.[18]

This understanding of how cognition builds experientially (that young learners are not empty vessels waiting to be filled, but living breathing crucibles of perception and experiences) extends established Vygotskyian principles of building new knowledge and skills on old ones, within the zone of proximal development of the child.[19] Learners are constantly updating their personal mental schema of the world built on their own experiences and perceptions, and learning to negotiate meaning with those around them.

Another key area of study for human social development is Theory of Mind (ToM). In considering the benefits for deaf young people of theatre-based practice, we added ToM development to our thinking, since studies suggest that access to language and language interactions are important in developing ToM reasoning. Theory of Mind, the recognition and naming of one's own and others' thoughts and feelings, seems to relate naturally to plays, plots and characters, and the very act of taking part in drama activities may help develop it. Carol Westby and Lee Robinson[20] identify the various stages and orders of ToM. The first order is the ability to think about what someone else is thinking or feeling; the second order includes the ability to think about what someone is thinking or feeling about what someone else is thinking or feeling; higher levels involve the recognition of lies, sarcasm, figurative language idioms and further multiple embeddings of thinking or feeling.

To apply this to Shakespeare in a workshop situation is to consider, for example, how Macbeth's thoughts and feelings may be both similar and different to your own. Through actively inhabiting the character of Macbeth, you instinctively make decisions about how that character is thinking and feeling. You understand that Macbeth has thoughts and feelings as you do, but also some thoughts and feelings that you (hopefully) don't have, and you can begin to consider and perhaps understand why such powerful thoughts and feelings arise in him. Shakespeare's plays also contain dramatic irony, for example when a character voices one thing to another character but tells the audience something quite different, or in the way in which the audience often knows something that a character does not, and has to hold both these thoughts in their mind at once. The levels of ToM needed to understand a play like *Macbeth* are thus quite complex.

While we did not find any published work on drama and ToM with deaf children, we were inspired by the work of Helen Chilton, who works on the use of picture books in developing ToM, particularly through creative writing activities with deaf children.[21] In consultations with Helen, we discussed how drama and, in particular, Shakespeare might be a productive avenue for looking further at this topic.

The principles of co-constructive pedagogy common to theatre-based practice, along with ToM, Helen Chilton's work, embodied cognition and a knowledge of the developmental issues facing deaf children and the wide range of what being 'deaf' can mean, all fed into a theoretical framework informing how we then worked with deaf practitioners and students and teachers of the deaf to create Shakespeare workshops for deaf young people.

Working with deaf practitioners was crucial in developing our understanding of the bridges to be discovered in communicating across hearing and deaf cultures, particularly in terms of increasing focus on visual rather than oral communication. Our first practical stage was a week of R&D on *Macbeth* in the summer of 2018. Our team included deaf actors and BSL interpreters. The aim for the week was to explore workshop activities that could be accessible and useful to deaf learners using oral/aural communication and those predominantly using sign language. Informed by our consultations with teachers of the deaf, we set out to devise activities guided by pedagogical principles familiar to such teachers:

- Appeal to the visual sense;
- Keep attention and interest and establish understanding quickly;
- Reduce cognitive overload;
- Learn by doing;
- Establish 'the known' and build on it.

'Building the heath' offers an example of how we put the principles set out above into practice. A 'heath', as in the place where Shakespeare's witches plan to meet Macbeth, does not have a clear equivalent in BSL. The 'translation' of Shakespeare into sign language necessitates a physical and contextual understanding of a word for understanding its meaning. To gain an understanding of the heath we developed an activity that began by showing a visual image of a misty landscape with trees and birds. Referring to this image, we could then ask the students what they could see, what else might be found there and how it might feel to be there. In practice with students, these questions allowed us to quickly establish their current understanding and references and then develop a shared understanding of what the heath might be like. Their descriptive suggestions moved from literal (trees, rocks, toads) to abstract (cold, lonely, scary) to a sense of the supernatural (mysterious, witches, zombies). We built on this understanding by physically making the scene, with students becoming their own suggestions: trees, birds, zombies and so on. Next, we added more atmosphere to this scene by adapting a 'soundscape' exercise of the weather. Rather than encouraging students to create sounds of wind, rain and thunder, we encouraged them to embody the wind, rain, thunder and lightning through visual and kinaesthetic cues.

One of the highlights of the R&D week was a performance of the opening scene of *Macbeth* with the witches using BSL, SSE and a highly physical theatrical form called Visual Vernacular (VV) that combines iconic BSL signs, facial expression, movement and gesture.[22] The importance of deaf young people being able to see key Shakespearean scenes performed by deaf artists, both in terms of seeing themselves represented on stage and reinforcing the idea that Shakespeare is for them, became clear. Having a scene performed in this way also modelled how the students could own the text for themselves and bring their own creative understanding to interpreting Shakespeare's language.

That week was an intensive but highly productive learning experience for us and we emerged with a real sense of mission that the project was worth continuing for the value it could contribute to young people's school experiences of Shakespeare. Building on the creative discoveries of the R&D week, we set about devising a two-part workshop to introduce the first act of *Macbeth* to deaf learners. We focused on story, character (particularly inhabiting character and understanding different perspectives) and vocabulary. We also introduced features of the language including metre, antithesis, metaphor, simile, imagery and personification, aspects that sign language can often express very vividly. Aware of the different communication modes and abilities of deaf learners, we were keen to try out our materials in a range of settings. Subsequently we trialled these workshops with students from three schools for the deaf, working with learners between the ages of 9 and 15 and with a range of communication methods and sometimes additional needs. While we had initially thought that the activities for each group might be quite different, it became increasingly apparent that all the learners could benefit from exercises that reinforced with visual stimuli, involved the use of the whole body in communication and invited and encouraged the use of sign.

Our iterative revisions of the workshops were mainly around doing more of what worked well and less of what didn't, rather than substantial changes to content, but we had learned a great deal about setting up exercises and sharing discoveries with deaf learners. For example, we found games of becoming soldiers and physically creating the events of the battle between Scotland and Norway at the start of the play very useful, both to tap into students' embodied cognition to establish the context for Macbeth's actions, and also to establish the discipline of working in an open space for learners unfamiliar with such practice. We realised the importance of scaffolding small steps if we were to ensure clarity of plot sequence, which allowed us to explore how such activities could support the ToM issues of who knows what and when in the play.

A core part of the initial workshops was a pilot film we commissioned of the witches' opening scene. Building on the performance from the R&D week, described above, three deaf actors created three versions of the witches' first scene in BSL, SSE and what we have termed Visual Shakespeare in acknowledgement of the influence of VV. All the young people were captivated by seeing that film and had no difficulty picking up the idea of creating their own versions of the scene. After watching the film, we asked the students to work in groups and asked each group to take on the lines of one of the witches to create their own performance through whatever combination of sign, gesture and sound they chose. Some signs or gestures were taken directly from the film, others were adapted, others still were invented anew. This resulted in a range of playful performances from functional to lyrical and even comical, as one group showed the setting of the sun with a blazer thrown over the sign for the sun. When we asked pairs to show 'fair' and 'foul', the range of signs and gestures demonstrated the deliberate ambiguity and multiplicity of meaning inherent in Shakespeare's line 'fair is foul and foul is fair' – a line all too often chanted without great thought. Some signed 'fair' as 'beautiful', some as 'just'; some signed 'foul' as 'ugly' or 'disgusting', some as a transgression in football.

Another interesting activity from the R&D week had involved visual illustrations of part of the plot. Exploring this alongside the influence of Helen Chilton's research with storybooks[23] inspired us to include a storyboard image of the offstage battle between Scotland and Norway in our trial workshops. The students were asked to become the Scottish court with King Duncan, his two sons, and their servants and attendants. The workshop leader then entered 'in role' as the Thane of Ross, and rather than verbally conveying the events of the battle, as one might do in a hearing classroom, offered the storybook image. Pairs were then tasked with working out what the message was from the image sequence. Having earlier enacted the battle, it took the students little time to decipher the meaning of the images, and to suggest the King's reaction – 'I am pleased we have won', 'I am happy with Macbeth', 'I am angry with the Thane of Cawdor'. The success of this exercise inspired us to include further storyboard images and illustrations in our complete scheme of work.

The least successful activity we trialled was using a clip from the 'live broadcast' film of the 2018 RSC production to convey the witches' prophecies to Macbeth and Banquo. The film clip included a BSL interpreter signing in a corner of the screen as well as subtitles, all on top of action that was often hard to make out in detail because it was quite dark. When we showed this to the students it quickly became apparent that the (very dark) action with subtitles and signing that was fast and sophisticated had transgressed our principle of avoiding cognitive overload, and we lost their attention. Their disconnection to this film was in marked contrast to the attention and enjoyment they had shown to the specially created film. It was an important moment for us, not only in reinforcing the issues around cognitive overload, but also in confirming the importance of putting films with deaf actors and creatives at the heart of our project.

As a last exercise in the two-part workshop, we trialled a 'writing-in-role' exercise influenced by the work of Chilton et al. on the evidence of ToM in the writing of deaf children. After embodying Macbeth and Banquo receiving the witches' prophesies, the students were asked to write letters home to their respective wives. Establishing any robust evidence of impact needs far more work, but we hoped to see signs that embodying a character helps learners to engage with that character's thoughts and feelings when writing in the first person. As well as showing a keen understanding of the complexities of the plot, the students were able to identify the feelings of Banquo and Macbeth: 'At this very moment, I'm confused'; 'I'm very happy about being made Thane of Cawdor'; 'I and Macbeth are confused seeing what is going to happen and we are both trying to think about it'; and even to project what Banquo or Macbeth might think that their wives were thinking: 'Dear my lovely Teddie Bear, I know you might be worried about me (from the battle)', 'Dear Gorgeous Wife, Please don't worry about me getting hurt I am fine'. This encouraged us to include more written exercises springing out of being in role in our final scheme of work.

The principles we set out with at the start of the R&D week served us well in creating, delivering and reviewing the trial workshops. We learned that the use of production film clips for deaf learners had to be carefully thought through, but that signed performances should be at the heart of our resources. We learned that a strong focus on visual and kinaesthetic modes of learning seemed effective and engaging. Displaying instructions and questions on screen and using props, such as sashes and crowns, as signifiers of character that could also chart the transferal of power from one person to another, seemed effective in easing cognitive load, as did PowerPoint images that reinforced the visual sense of location and identity (a picture of a heath for the first scene, maps showing Scotland and Norway, images of the Scottish and Norwegian flags). Embodying the battle through active collaborative exercises maintained attention and enjoyment, which helped to build understanding of the importance of the battle and of the betrayal of the Thane of Glamis (only reported in the play).

Reviewing all our learning, we put films by deaf actors at the heart of the scheme of work we went on to create for the whole play. One of our first actions was to identify ten key moments across the whole play and commission filmed performances of each moment. Each film was performed by a deaf actor in BSL, with most versions additionally in SSE, and some in Visual Shakespeare to inspire students to create their own versions. We were fortunate to be able to work with some brilliant professional deaf artists including RSC Associate Artist Charlotte Arrowsmith and RSC actor William Grint as our directors. We were also delighted to have three deaf students from Braidwood School play the Apparitions in the films of the second set of prophecies. These students spent a day working with Charlotte and hearing actor and interpreter Becky Barry to devise and film their performances. Around each film, we have created a package of activities and resources designed for deaf learners to support their study and enjoyment of the whole play of *Macbeth*.

There are two versions of the scheme of work available on the RSC website. While all activities are the same, one version includes films in BSL with deaf actors from the UK, and the other includes films in ASL (American Sign Language) with deaf actors from the US. We were awarded funding from the Billy Rose Foundation in New York to create these ASL films and are deeply grateful to Lindsey Snyder and her team for making these films happen.

Our project, like so many others, was interrupted by the pandemic and suffered an eighteen-month hiatus. It is worth saying, however, that even before then we had to balance our ideals with limitations on time and resources. We hope that this project will seed interest so that in future we can find funding to tip the balance more in favour of our ideals, which are to work more closely with deaf practitioners, artists and technicians and spend more time trialling the activities and assessing the impact of the work with teachers of the deaf and their students. We hope that our project can promote not just increased deaf awareness but appreciation of how deaf artists and young people can bring new ideas and interpretations to working with Shakespeare for us all. We hope teachers across the world will access the resources from the RSC website, be inspired to trial them and feed back to us about impact and ideas for further development.

In summary, the five key principles we established to underpin Signing Shakespeare are:

1. Closely following the chronology of the narrative. This means trusting that Shakespeare gives us what we need when we need it. So we need to meet the witches to set the atmosphere and build anticipation of Macbeth, then experience the battle as described to Duncan, then hear Duncan's response with his praise of Macbeth, and his decision to execute the Thane of Cawdor and reward Macbeth with that title. This order stimulates the audience's ToM so that they can enjoy the dramatic irony of different characters knowing different things at different times.

2. Using explicit visual resources. Visual aids support cognitive ease and promote understanding – for example, using images to reinforce ideas, characters and places, and sashes to indicate character and the transferal of power from one person to another.

3. Using performance techniques and kinaesthetic learning. Through inhabiting characters – playing Macbeth, Banquo, Duncan, the witches, etc. – we tapped into the students' embodied cognition. This included inhabiting settings, for example the soldiers in the battle or images of the heath where the witches first meet.

4. Reinforcing cumulative knowledge and exploring interpretations. We reinforced cumulative knowledge through closed questions such as 'Who do the witches plan to meet?' and explored interpretations through open questions such as 'What do you think it feels like to be in this place?'

5. Short films created by deaf artists for deaf students. All the students were highly engaged in watching the bespoke films we created for key moments in the narrative. The skilled actors provide role models. They not only support the students' understanding but inspire them to create their own versions, and perhaps raise their aspirations for what they themselves can achieve.

Tracy Irish is an experienced teacher, theatre practitioner and scholar with a specialism in Shakespeare. She has worked with a wide range of schools and theatre companies in the UK and internationally, and is an Associate Learning Practitioner with the Royal Shakespeare Company and a Visiting Lecturer for the universities of Birmingham and Warwick. She has authored a range of resources and publications including *RSC School Shakespeare* editions for Oxford University Press and *Shakespeare and Meisner* for the Arden Performance series. She is currently co-authoring *Teaching and Learning Shakespeare through Theatre-Based Practice* for Arden Shakespeare.

Abigail Rokison-Woodall began her career as a professional actor. She is now Deputy Director (Education) and Associate Professor at the Shakespeare Institute. Abigail has written a number of journal articles and chapters on Shakespeare and other drama. Her first monograph, *Shakespearean Verse Speaking* (Cambridge University Press, 2010), won the inaugural Shakespeare's Globe first book award. She has published three more books: *Shakespeare for Young People: Productions, Versions and Adaptations* (Bloomsbury Arden, 2013), *Shakespeare in the Theatre: Nicholas Hytner* (Bloomsbury Arden, 2017) and *As You Like It: Language and Writing* (Bloomsbury Arden, 2021). She is the co-general editor with Michael Dobson and Simon Russell Beale of the Arden Shakespeare Performance Editions, for which she has edited *A Midsummer Night's Dream*, *Hamlet* and *King Lear* (the latter with Simon Russell Beale). She is also co-general editor of the Arden Shakespeare in Performance: A Practical Guide series, for which she is co-writing *Shakespeare and Lecoq*. She is currently working with RSC Education on a project about teaching Shakespeare to deaf children.

Notes

1. Debates about capitalising 'deaf' to indicate the distinct culture and community of deaf people are ongoing and we are fully respectful of that distinction. Because we are mainly talking about deaf young people in education, where capitalising deaf is less common, we have chosen not to capitalise throughout to avoid potential confusion.
2. RSC, 'Signing Shakespeare', https://www.rsc.org.uk/learn/schools-and-teachers/teacher-resources/signing-shakespeare-for-deaf-students (accessed 6 February 2023).
3. Our project focused on working with British Sign Language (BSL). With colleagues in the US we were able to add alternative films in American Sign Language (ASL). The activities can be adapted for use with other sign languages.
4. Robert Adams, 'Sign Language through the Ages', *The Essay*, BBC Radio 3, September 2022.
5. There is not room in this chapter, nor has there yet been time in our project, to sufficiently review research into the relationship between sign and learning, but for those interested in finding out more, a good place to start is the Deafness, Language and Cognition Research Centre (DCAL) at UCL.
6. British Deaf Association, 'Deaf Roots and Pride', https://bda.org.uk/project/deafrootspride/ (accessed 23 January 2023).
7. National Deaf Children's Society, 'Consortium for Research in Deaf Education: 2021 UK-Wide Summary', https://www.ndcs.org.uk/media/7842/cride-2021-uk-wide-summary-final.pdf (accessed 23 January 2023).
8. Robert Adams, 'Sign Language is My Language', *The Essay*, BBC Radio 3, September 2022.
9. Braidwood Trust School for the Deaf, 'Total Communication', https://www.braidwood.bham.sch.uk/page/?title=Total+Communication&pid=36 (accessed 23 January 2023).
10. Deaf Museums in Europe, 'History of Deaf People in Europe: Education, Sign Language Recognition, Politics and More', https://www.deafhistory.eu/index.php/deaf-history (accessed 23 January 2023).
11. National Deaf Children's Society, 'Consortium'.
12. Jacqui O'Hanlon and Angie Wootten, *Using Drama to Teach Personal, Social and Emotional Skills* (London: SAGE, 2017).
13. See, for example: H. Cayton, 'The Contribution of Drama to the Education of Deaf Children', *Journal of British Association of Teachers of the Deaf* 18(3) (1981), 43–48; A. Seeley and J. Camus, 'Developing an Approach to Drama with Hearing Impaired Children', *Journal of British Association of Teachers of the Deaf* 7(2) (1983), 30–34.
14. British Association of Teachers of Deaf Children and Young People, 'NDCS Update – Deaf Pupils Achieve an Entire GCSE Grade Less for Sixth Year Running', 6 August 2021, https://www.batod.org.uk/ndcs-update-deaf-pupils-achieve-an-entire-gcse-grade-less-for-sixth-year-running/ (accessed 23 January 2023).
15. RSC, 'Research into Our Work', https://www.rsc.org.uk/learn/research-into-our-work (accessed 23 January 2023).
16. RSC, *The RSC Shakespeare Toolkit for Teachers* (London: Methuen Drama, 2010).

17. Lawrence Shapiro and Steven A. Stolz, 'Embodied Cognition and Its Significance for Education', *Theory and Research in Education* 17(1) (2019): 19–39, 26.
18. Cicely Berry, 'Foreword', in James Stredder, *The North Face of Shakespeare* (Cambridge: Cambridge University Press, 2009), viii–x, viii.
19. Lev Vygotsky, *Mind in Society: The Development of Higher Psychological Processes* (Cambridge, MA: Harvard University Press, 1978), 102.
20. Carol Westby and Lee Robinson, 'A Developmental Perspective for Promoting Theory of Mind', *Topics in Language Disorders* 34 (2014), 362–82.
21. Helen Chilton, 'Tricks, Lies and Mistakes: Identifying Theory of Mind Concepts within Storybooks with Deaf Children', *Deafness and Education International* 19(2) (2017), 75–78; Helen Chilton, Connie Mayer and Wendy McCracken, 'Evidence of Theory of Mind in the Writing of Deaf Children', *Journal of Deaf Studies and Deaf Education* 24(1) (2019), 32–40.
22. Visual Vernacular is a term coined by American deaf actor Bernard Bragg. It sits somewhere in between sign language, sign poetry and visual art. It has its own complexities and rules.
23. Chilton, 'Tricks, Lies and Mistakes'.

Chapter 9
A World Elsewhere
Documentary Representations of Social Shakespeare

Susanne Greenhalgh

Documentaries on radio and television are important ways in which the concepts and practices of applied Shakespeare are disseminated and popularised. However, such 'reality Shakespeare' recordings are never neutral documentations, but rather transcode performance into the conventions of broadcast narrative and presentation. This is particularly evident when programmes deal with the redemptive value of performing Shakespeare with disadvantaged social groups, such as prisoners or young people in deprived, often ethnic communities, or those in need of therapeutic interventions, such as soldiers post-conflict or those with learning disabilities. As Sheila Preston observes while considering the 'ethics of representation' in applied theatre, 'such representations of the disenfranchised can so easily become a problematic commodity'.[1] In order to interrogate 'the choices that are made in applied theatre texts, for, with and by communities

Notes for this section begin on page 159.

in particular social and particular contexts',[2] attention must be paid to how these texts are represented in the media that bring them to our attention. Equally, in order to determine the ideological inflection of broadcast representations of applied Shakespeare in different social or therapeutic contexts, the circumstances in which these media representations were made and disseminated must be given due consideration. As archives of approaches to such work, these media outputs appear to provide valuable documentation for those – students, scholars, practitioners – for whom such recordings may be the only source for viewing a company's application of Shakespeare in practice. But they are perhaps even more valuable as advertising for the claimed effects on participants, and thus to invite or justify funding, as well as validating the chosen methods. And when these documentations are the subject of academic inquiry, it is essential to heed Courtney Lehmann's warning that this academic critique can all too easily become a form of 'anthropological exploitation' based on second-hand knowledge of the populations depicted.[3]

As Helen Nicholson has explored, the linkage of the term 'applied' with theatre or drama in order to identify a specific mode of performative engagement is a relatively new phenomenon, coming into general use only during the 1990s,[4] but having its origins in three pre-existing strands of theatrical practice:

> theatres of the political Left, which have been variously described as political, radical or alternative; drama and theatre in education; and community theatre. Taken together, they offer a powerful legacy which links social and personal change to dramatic practice, and articulate a commitment to using theatre to break down social hierarchies and divisions. What these traditions share is an interest in working in clearly defined contexts, with and for specific audiences, and in furthering objectives which are not only artistic, but also educational, social and political. Although differently inflected, all practitioners in applied drama are in some way indebted to these complementary histories.[5]

Writing specifically about the role of Shakespeare in representations of such work, Matt Kozusko gives examples of the enacted narratives of discovery, authenticity and validation that they perpetuate:

> A timid student shines triumphantly as he recites a passage from Hamlet; a terrified understudy conquers her fears on a successful opening night; a guilt-stricken prisoner turns out an improbably forceful performance of a penitent murderer: at-risk or otherwise

challenged populations give themselves over to Shakespeare and thereby discover within themselves a powerful humanity, an occluded potential, a fundamental innocence that they and the witnessing audience need to see authenticated. A deficit of some sort is established and then resolved with recourse to Shakespeare, whose power to capture or describe humanity turns out also to have the power to discover and validate humanity.[6]

Although the work of British psychiatrist Murray Cox at Broadmoor was documented in print in 1992,[7] and the Shakespeare Behind Bars (SBB) prison project in the USA began the same year, academic interest in the application of Shakespeare in these contexts really took off during the first decades of the twenty-first century, partly fed by films and broadcasts documenting performance projects, some of which were shown at international Shakespeare conferences. There is now a steady stream of publications and a number of university courses devoted to this aspect of Shakespeare studies. To date, however, there is no agreed terminology for 'applied Shakespeare'. Contextualising it as an aspect of amateur theatre, Michael Dobson termed it 'voluntary sector Shakespeare' in the seminar he convened at the 2012 Shakespeare Association Conference in Boston, and stressed its relation to civic values.[8] Michael P. Jensen labels it 'Service Shakespeare' in his follow-up special issue of *Borrowers and Lenders*, but offers a plenitude of questions about this taxonomy in place of a definition.[9] My own preferred term of 'Social Shakespeare' is indebted to the definitions that James Thompson and Richard Schechner derive from the work of the Italian theatre worker Guglielmo Schininà. Schininà argues that social theatre differs from other forms of theatrical-therapeutic techniques, such as dramatherapy, in its objective 'to question society, with the living presence of its differences, rather than to be purified, and brought back to a "normal" value system or social code'.[10] For Thompson and Schechner such practices put social work and theatre in dynamic interaction so that 'change can come to both disciplines'.[11]

The 'Shakestherapy' broadcasting genre with its rules of 'emotional authenticity underwritten by Shakespeare; redemption by Shakespeare',[12] is associated both with the factual documenting of social problems and issues, purporting to offer 'reality' in an objective way, and with an anthropologically focused exploration of otherness. However, its narratives often invite audiences to engage emotionally with the journey undertaken by the objects of study, making it comparable to genres like melodrama (viewed as a conservative mode of theatre exploiting the pathos of the deserving disadvantaged for sentimental effect). To make the journey more vivid, contrasts are frequently set up, aurally or visually, between the initial environment, or the performers' original situation, and the 'magic' or 'safe space' represented by theatre. Rob Pensalfini labels this the 'sanctified space' of Shakespeare,[13] while Kozusko characterises it as 'a kind of empty space, sacred and sanctioned, in which a particular kind of therapeutic narrative unfolds independent of semantic particulars'.[14] His echoing of Peter Brook – theatre comes into being when an actor is watched entering an empty space – alerts us to the vital role of the audience in the sanctioning of the therapeutic effects of performance that are relayed to them.

The requirements of commissioning, editing and scheduling documentary films and broadcasts tend towards formats that bookend stories of achievement rather than failure, through depictions of the obstacles successfully overcome on the way to achieving an applauded final performance. This often takes place in theatres that are labelled as 'professional' even when the audience consists of invited friends and family rather than a paying public. Such representations mirror mainstream media's normalising of physical and mental disability or trauma through depiction of an individual triumphing 'against all odds'. A dominant feature of both the performances and the recordings is the idea that performers can find their experience mirrored in Shakespeare's characters and that the process of rehearsal exploration of the themes of specific plays can transform the personal state of the actors. According to Jensen, these 'parallels help non-actors give compelling performances'.[15] However, Kozusko considers that such 'authentic' self-identifications are often actually grounded in the misreadings inevitably generated by the opacity of Shakespeare's language. In such instances, a prisoner can be 'transported from the position of player in a performance of *Hamlet* to a space of solitary penance' because he, the director and audience experience Claudius's momentary repentance as genuine, although his final words – 'Words without thoughts never to heaven go' (*Hamlet*, 3.3.98)[16] – refute this.[17] Moreover, such emotional involvement also ensures that attention focuses on personalities, in ways typical of other reality shows that make entertainment out of taking individuals into spheres outside their comfort zone As Geoffrey Ridden observes, 'this practice of "character criticism" may be essential to an agenda not only of personal rehabilitation but also social reintegration',[18] but the resulting 'narrative[s] of individual transcendence'[19] also run the risk of endorsing an ideology that locates transformation in the individual, rather than society.

Rather, the 'communal' experience of theatre is itself constructed as a social microcosm, a 'little world' in which disputes and personal conflicts (often centred on issues of gender, racial or sexual identity) are overcome in the service of the collective imperative that the 'show must go on'. While a director or facilitator is usually at times in evidence, and included in the talking-head sequences that are obligatory, there is rarely any overt disclosure or discussion of the specific forms of drama activity or concepts drawn upon in their work. Instead, in some programmes the appearance of celebrity visitors or mentors as guides on the journey, or as helpful *dei ex machina* who act as Shakespeare's representatives on earth, further endorse his works in utopian terms as a resource for aspiration and rehabilitation.[20] In order to consider how far such documentations convey the 'living presence' of society's differences, I examine three examples focused on three different constituencies: prisoners, young people with learning disabilities, and combat veterans.

The award-winning 2005 film *Shakespeare Behind Bars*, directed by Hank Rogerson, is probably the best-known example of the genre, and also the one most used in teaching. Filmed over a year, in 2003, it follows the work of prisoners in the Luther Luckett Correctional Complex in Oldham County, Kentucky, on a production of *The Tempest*, the fourth of a sequence of Shakespeare productions on the theme of forgiveness.[21] In the timeline of the film, the prisoners, most of whom are experienced members of the project from previous years, are often shown working on their own and casting themselves in the roles that 'call' to them, as is the rule for performances which are designed to mirror the crimes or other emotional traumas of the actors' pre-prison lives. Against a *mise en scène* of the banal everyday life of the jail, the documentary deliberately parallels the prisoners' direct-to-camera reflections on the past crimes that have brought them to the penitentiary with the crime/exile/revenge narrative of *The Tempest* and its thematic stress on forgiveness, reconciliation and freedom. The project founder, Curt Tofteland, claims that 'habilitation' rather than rehabilitation is its objective, implying that its processes aim at 'enabling or endowing with ability or fitness'.[22] What remains opaque is whether the prisoners are being prepared for life outside, as the Prison Governor claims, or for the reality of continuing detention.

When present, Tofteland is shown briefly conducting theatre exercises to create group identity and verbal dexterity, but is most often seen sitting to one side as scenes are rehearsed, his interventions typically urging the actors towards finding 'truth' through emotionally charged performance. One actor seemingly achieves this objective when his performance of Henry V's Agincourt speech ends in the 'authenticity' of a tearful embrace of a fellow inmate, and Caliban is urged to stoke up more and more anger to fuel his cursing of Prospero. The extent to which the most seasoned actors have absorbed this Method-like approach is evident in a rehearsal scene, when the actor playing Miranda, who has earlier revealed that this was not his choice of role, resists direction by Prospero to connect his performance with his personal history of parental loss. The obstacles encountered during the rehearsal process thus include the ways in which the problematics of sexuality in an all-male prison environment are heightened by cross-gender casting. However, those posed by the penal system itself, such as the tension around whether the parole application of one of the founding members will succeed, or the impact of actors being sent to solitary in the 'Hole', are either accepted as part of the habitat of what the Prison Governor describes as an 'island', or aestheticised through recurring images of bars and surveillance contrasted with shots of sky and clouds, that, together with the annotated play scripts, come to represent the 'dream' of freedom.

The film also picks up on *The Tempest*'s concern with theatre. Prison life itself is described by some inmates as a site of constant acting, and thus inauthenticity, so that their theatrical performances become a prompt for truthful self-reflection and what Tofteland and inmate Hal Cobb (who plays Prospero in the play) call 'a metamorphosis of the heart'. Writing from the perspective of identifying a 'penitential' strand in Shakespeare's writing, one that can support a process of recognition and repentance for prison inmates through engagement with Shakespearean language, Neils Herold and Matt Wallace argue that

> the complete immersion of the player's self in a role he has felt called upon to enact appears to generate *a truthfulness through doubleness*, which allows the inmate to acknowledge his crimes and win back the acceptance of his humanity.[23]

The enhanced articulacy credited to the learning and speaking of Shakespeare's language is construed as inmates being able to 'speak what they feel' (*King Lear*, 5.3.300) rather than hiding emotionally behind codes of violent, criminal masculinity. Unlike in the other films, the final performance remains confined within the prison precincts, played on a makeshift though colourful set, before an audience of invited guests. Although we are told that the play was performed for fellow inmates and toured to other prisons, the film does not show these performances. The film constructs a 'dream' of redemption out of a production that is the culmination of a series of plays featuring forgiveness, but *The Tempest*'s final words, a plea to be set free, inevitably take on an ironic edge, since the continued life of the project is premised on the continuing imprisonment of the cast. Pensalfini notes in his history of prison Shakespeare that mainstream media gives greater attention to this form compared with other types of drama activity behind bars, often in the form of short packages on local TV stations.[24] Implicitly or explicitly, this media coverage engages with questions about crime and punishment, and controversies about rehabilitating prisoners through access to educative and socialising experiences. However, such debates are typically framed in moral rather than ideological terms: Shakespeare's texts are appropriate because his characters are conceived of first and foremost as moral agents. Unsurprisingly, *Shakespeare Behind Bars* makes a powerful case for the value of Shakespeare as a humanising force in a dehumanising context, but it does so by accepting the inevitability of incarceration, framing Shakespearean performance as moral instruction, vehicle of individual catharsis, and as a temporary escape to a world elsewhere.

Growing Up Down's is a 60-minute British documentary, directed by William Jessop, and shown on BBC Three in 2015. It documents a production of *Hamlet* by the Winchester-based theatre company Blue Apple. The company was founded by William's mother, Jane Jessop in 2005, while she was Chair of Winchester Mencap, and its mission is to 'support performers with learning difficulties to develop and present high quality productions to the widest possible audience'.[25] In addition to *Hamlet*, they have mounted productions of *A Midsummer Night's Dream* (2010) and *Much Ado about Nothing* (2014), which have toured to venues in the south of England. William Jessop adapted *Hamlet* for a one-hour performance and his brother, Tommy, who has Down's Syndrome, plays the prince, having already established an acting career in television and film. The film is thus a family affair and benefits from the relaxed intimacy this brings to the filming. Unlike the other films discussed, the director makes his presence evident, not only as narrator, but by introducing himself reflected in a mirror near the start. The direct-to-camera inserts sometimes include his off-camera questions or comments, and at one point, when tempers flare violently in rehearsal, the camera swings out of control as he attempts to defuse the situation. Like *Shakespeare Behind Bars*, *Growing Up Down's* was nominated for and won awards.

The opening title sequence starts with an image of Tommy Jessop climbing onto the stage of an ornate nineteenth-century theatre and delivering the first five lines of the 'To be, or not to be' soliloquy. Over footage of a car journey William Jessop's voiceover tells us that the film will follow these 'extraordinary young actors', four of whom – Tommy, Katie, Lawrie and James – are introduced by name in the sequences that follow, and will be the focus throughout. The narration states that the film will show how 'along the way the play will blur with their real lives' and take them on a 'roller coaster ride of romance, rows, and revelations', ending with the question, 'Can they really pull off Shakespeare's *Hamlet*?' However, the film, as the title suggests, also seeks to encapsulate the rites of passage these young people undergo as they embark on adult life with Down's Syndrome or other learning disabilities. Although Shakespeare's tragedy is their medium, the film's focus is equally on their desires for a future in which they can enjoy successful relationships and fulfilling employment. We see them making music or dancing in their homes, and Tommy in particular is filmed several times in the pastoral setting of the South Downs countryside. What is narratively framed as a first kiss between him and Katie takes place on camera in woodland, and he releases tension about his performance in a shout that sends a flock of birds scattering against the sky. As with *Shakespeare Behind Bars*, such deliberately aesthetic choices in the cinematography endow the film with an aura of quality that echoes that represented by Shakespeare.

As is typical of such films the majority of sequences deal with the rehearsal process and the encounters and emotions this generates. However, very little camera time is given to the director, Peter Clerke, who has a background in community theatre. Tommy is the charismatic centre of attraction for his brother's camera, as he is for both Lawrie and Katy, and many of the emotional issues that are probed in the film concern the resulting tensions and readjustments in their relationships with each other. Early on, William Jessop comments: 'When Tommy first started acting, he found it hard to separate the fictional storylines from real life. I've also noticed this in other actors with Down's'. The film continually presents us with scenes in which the emotional states of the actors mirror those of the characters. Lawrie, for example, links the play's preoccupation with death with his own personal history of loss. At times the actors are shown trying to change the script to bring it into line with their preoccupations. Katie, who plays Ophelia, argues for a happy ending in which she and Hamlet marry, an alteration that Lawrie, playing Claudius, resists on the grounds that it would no longer be Shakespeare's tragedy.

An important narrative strand in the film is its depiction of the cast's growing confidence that they are actors playing parts, not the characters they portray. This is signalled as a vital part of the 'growing up' which is the film's main theme. Early on in the film, the cast are taken to the Normansfield Theatre, created in the nineteenth century by John Langdon Down (from whom the syndrome takes its name) after he observed his patients' liking for acting. Once the production moves from rehearsal room to sequences of the theatre tour, we see successively more polished performances, culminating in the curtain call on the stage of the Rose Theatre in Kingston. Prior to *Hamlet*, William Jessop wrote a short play, *Living Without Fear*, which tackled disability hate crime, and was performed at the Speaker's House at Westminster for government ministers and Members of Parliament. The line given the most emphasis in the film's portrayal of Hamlet's 'To be or not to be' soliloquy is 'And lose the name of action' (3.1.90). Although *Growing Up Down's* privileges the emotional engagement of its young actors, immersion in their roles is temporary and valued as a means to an agency which is social and outward-facing. The sanctified space of Shakespeare is depicted as opening out into future opportunities, both professional and personal.

My final example considers the media representation of the work of the Combat Veteran Players (CVP), founded in London in 2009 by Jaclyn McLoughlin. Productions to date are *A Midsummer Night's Dream*, *Henry V*, *Richard III* and *Twelfth Night*, and in addition to support from the veterans' charity STOLL, the company has received sponsorship and performance opportunities from the Royal Shakespeare Company, Shakespeare's Globe and the British

Council.²⁶ Although the first productions were all-male, ex-service women are now included, with the proviso that all actors must have suffered from combat trauma or mental distress, so that there is an equality of experience. The mission statement published on their website describes CVP as 'an award-winning Shakespearean theatre company of ex-Servicemen and women making professional level theatre while overcoming injury or transitional difficulty'.²⁷ Unlike the previous two case studies, the recordings of CVP's work were made-for television and radio features rather than full-length documentary films. One is a half-hour BBC Radio 4 feature, *And Calm of Mind*, directed by Chris Ledgard and broadcast the day before Shakespeare's traditional birthday in 2013.²⁸ The other is a fifteen-minute package within the London weekly magazine programme *Inside Out* on BBC1, recorded in 2014.²⁹ Both provide further evidence of the media's penchant for stories that combine therapy and Shakespeare, in these instances also responding to public concern for the military following Britain's involvement in the second Iraq War and the war in Afghanistan.

A former actor, McLoughlin first explored the idea of drama work with soldiers suffering from post-traumatic stress disorder theoretically, in an MA essay, and embarked on a PhD on the topic. She switched to putting her ideas into practice under the guidance of Dr Walter Busuttil, Director of Medical Services for the charity Combat Stress, which helps former service members struggling with mental health difficulties. Although McLoughlin emphasises that she is not a dramatherapist but a theatre director, her work is described as therapeutic both by the participants and in the media, and she cites Freud on trauma to argue that 'touching' the emotions of another may be therapeutic. In the *Inside Out* film, she states: 'a lot of what I work with is identity. I think there's a lot of lost identity that happens when you're transitioning from combat into civilian'. McLoughlin's concern with identity echoes the ideas enshrined in the Military Covenant which from 2000 outlined 'the mutual obligations between the Nation, the Army and each individual soldier: an unbreakable common bond of identity, loyalty and responsibility which has sustained the Army throughout its history'.³⁰

The radio feature takes its title from Milton, not Shakespeare, using part of the final line of *Samson Agonistes*, after he has triumphed over his enemies: 'And calm of mind all passion spent'.³¹ It deals with rehearsals for *Henry V* and much is made of how the play's concern with war may be problematic for men who have encountered its horrors in reality. The 'calm' that can be attained through Shakespeare is attributed to the 'richness' and 'timelessness' of his language. The programme exploits the aural soundscape of group performance and intimate revelation to emphasise the way that an ethos of solidarity enables individuals to come to terms with their experiences, through forms of theatrical distancing such as the division of the role of Henry between all eight actors. One describes how his depression has been helped by playing 'both sides' of the war experience, both the Boy, viewed as a helpless victim, and Henry, the leader needing to stay strong for his men. The participants' emotional memory is directed into a performance mode that externalises and shares the guilts and consequences of war through ensemble performance, while accepting that there may be no complete resolution for the individual.

The *Inside Out* television package also revisits the work on *Henry V*, juxtaposing workshop and talking-head sequences with footage from the Bosnian and Iraq wars, but also looks forward to a production of *Hamlet* at Shakespeare's Globe, enabling footage of the actors visiting that iconic and photogenic stage. Unlike the less naturalistic and introspective approach to character evidently taken in *Henry V*, the actor cast as Hamlet connects the prince's suicidal thoughts with his own, while another seems to echo the play's atmospherics when he recalls how 'a number of incidents ... come back to me in my dreams. They queue up like ghosts from the past and come visit in the night'. Countering these confessions of mental distress, the trope that the theatre ensemble is a replacement 'band of brothers' (*Henry V*, 4.3.60) threads through both broadcasts. Both culminate with a theatre performance or the promise of one, but there is no indication that the productions will offer a critique of the military institution or the political policies that govern its deployment. Although the camaraderie of the performance process may indeed calm the veterans' minds and aid their transition to civilian life, the trauma of war is regarded as an inevitable part of the covenant of military service, a service embellished by Shakespeare's language and theatricality.

While these recordings engage with Shakespeare applied to distinctly different social contexts and life stages, the similarity in their narrative structures is striking. All the projects aspire to be high-quality productions, for which Shakespeare is regarded as providing the best material. Apart from *Shakespeare Behind Bars*, this achievement of quality is signalled by performance in a 'real' theatre, preferably one with Shakespearean associations, ideally Shakespeare's Globe, or, as the next best thing, Kingston's Rose Theatre. All show the actors seeking and finding parallels to their own experience in Shakespeare's characters, though only *Growing Up Down's* suggests that this is an approach to acting that must be grown out of. What is often missing in such documentations is acknowledgement of the particular dramatic and therapeutic practices out of which the work is developed. Shakespeare is made to appear to be the 'onlie begetter' of any transformation that takes place. As Ridden observes, 'a film has to play safe and represent the therapy of high culture through the citing of Shakespeare, whether or not Shakespeare was indeed the therapy in real life'.[32] If, as Tim Prentki and Sheila Preston argue, 'Applied theatre denotes the intention to employ theatre processes in the service of self-development, well-being and social change',[33] the broadcasts examined here do indeed document the applying of Shakespeare in the service of self-development and well-being. However, when watching or teaching with such documentations, we should stay alert to the ways in which, whether or not the processes and performances represented themselves work towards social change, the narratives of these broadcasts tend to restore them to 'normal' value systems and social codes. The extent to which the Shakespeare they portray can be considered social theatre, as understood by Thompson and Schechner – both social work and theatre in dynamic interaction – remains an open question.

Susanne Greenhalgh is an Honorary Research Fellow in the School of Arts and Digital Industries, University of Roehampton. Her research interests centre on Shakespearean adaptation and reception, and the relationship between theatre, culture and audio-visual media. She has written many articles on Shakespeare's appropriation and citation in different periods and settings, including children's literature, television, radio and live broadcasts to cinema. With Kate Chedgzoy and Robert Shaughnessy she co-edited *Shakespeare and Childhood* (Cambridge University Press, 2007), and with Pascale Aebischer and Laurie Osborne, *Shakespeare and the 'Live' Theatre Broadcast Experience* (Arden Bloomsbury, 2018), as well as special issues of *Shakespeare* and *Shakespeare Bulletin*.

Notes

1. Sheila Preston, 'Introduction to Ethics of Representation', in *The Applied Theatre Reader*, ed. Tim Prentki and Sheila Preston (London: Routledge, 2008), 68.
2. Ibid.
3. Courtney Lehmann, 'Double Jeopardy: Shakespeare and Prison Theater', in *Shakespeare and the Ethics of Appropriation*, ed. Alexa Huang and Elizabeth Rivlin (Basingstoke: Palgrave Macmillan, 2014), 91.
4. Helen Nicholson, *Applied Drama: The Gift of Theatre* (Basingstoke: Palgrave Macmillan, 2005), 2.
5. Ibid., 8.
6. Matt Kozusko, 'Monstrous! Actors, Audiences, Inmates and the Politics of Reading Shakespeare', *Shakespeare Bulletin* 28, no. 2 (2010), 238.
7. Murray Cox, *Shakespeare Comes to Broadmoor: 'The Actors are Come Hither': The Performance of Tragedy in a Secure Psychiatric Hospital* (London: Jessica Kingsley, 1992).
8. See also his essay 'Shakespearean Comedy as a Way of Life: Performance and the Voluntary Sector', in *Shakespeare in Performance*, ed. Eric C. Brown and Estelle Rivier (Cambridge: Cambridge Scholars Publishing, 2014), 121–137.
9. Michael P. Jensen, '"What Service Is Here?" Exploring Service Shakespeare', *Borrowers and Lenders* 8, no. 2 (2013/14), n.p., http://www.borrowers.uga.edu/1039/show.
10. Guglielmo Schininà, 'Here We Are: Social Theatre and Some Open Questions about Its Developments', *TDR: The Drama Review* 48, no. 3 (2004), 24.
11. James Thompson and Richard Schechner, 'Why "Social Theatre"?', *TDR: The Drama Review* 48, no. 3 (2004), 13.
12. Kozusko, 'Monstrous!', 238.
13. Rob Pensalfini, *Prison Shakespeare: For These Deep Shames and Great Indignities* (Basingstoke: Palgrave, 2015), 20.
14. Kozusko, 'Monstrous!', 238.
15. Jensen, '"What Service Is Here?"', n.p.
16. All quotations from Shakespeare are taken from Stanley Wells and Gary Taylor, eds, *Shakespeare: The Complete Works* (Oxford: Clarendon Press, 1988).
17. Kozusko, 'Monstrous!', 238.
18. Geoffrey M. Ridden, 'The Bard's Speech: Making It Better; Shakespeare and Therapy on Film', *Borrowers and Lenders* 8, no. 2 (2013/14), n.p., http://www.borrowers.uga.edu/1015/show.
19. Lehmann, 'Double Jeopardy', 91.
20. See, for example, *The Hobart Shakespeareans* (dir. Mel Stuart, 2005) in which Ian McKellen and Michael York visit schoolchildren performing *Hamlet* in class; and *My Shakespeare* (dir. Michael Waldman, 2004), which features Baz Luhrmann mentoring disadvantaged young people in East London via Skype. For further discussion, see Susanne Greenhalgh and Robert Shaughnessy, 'Our Shakespeares: British Television and the Strains of Multiculturalism', in *Screening Shakespeare in the Twenty-First Century*, ed. Mark Thornton Burnett and Ramona Wray (Edinburgh: Edinburgh University Press, 2006), 90–112.
21. The previous productions were *Othello, Titus Andronicus* and *Hamlet*.

160 Susanne Greenhalgh

22. *Oxford English Dictionary* (Oxford: Oxford University Press, 1989) (accessed 2 October 2018).
23. Neils Herold and Matt Wallace, 'Time Served in Prison Shakespeare', *Selected Papers of the Ohio Valley Shakespeare Conference*, vol. 4, article 2 (2011), http://ideaexchange.uakron.edu/spovsc/vol4/iss2011/2.
24. Pensalfini, *Prison Shakespeare*, 89.
25. Blue Apple Theatre, http://blueappletheatre.com/ (accessed 12 November 2018).
26. McLoughlin has also worked with the United Service Organization (USO) in America directing *The Comedy of Errors* with US veterans in 2015. See Madaline Donnelly, 'Can Shakespeare Heal? One Director's Quest to Help PTSD', *The Daily Signal*, 7 September 2015, https://www.dailysignal.com/2015/09/07/can-shakespeare-heal-one-directors-quest-to-help-treat-ptsd/. In 2016, as part of the Shakespeare Lives programme of events in honour of the 400th anniversary of Shakespeare's death, *The Comedy of Errors* was performed by British and American veterans at the American Shakespeare Company's Lansburgh Theatre, in Washington DC.
27. Combat Veteran Players, http://www.combatveteranplayers.org.uk/ (accessed 12 November 2018). More recently, members of the company have collaborated with 'Shakespeare's Soldiers', founded by Amanda Faber to take workshops and performances into UK schools. Faber also set up the Soldier's Arts Academy as a platform for military personnel to participate in the creative and performing arts. See https://www.soldiersartsacademy.com/ (accessed 12 November 2018).
28. Available at https://www.bbc.co.uk/sounds/play/b01s09kf (accessed 12 November 2018).
29. Part of this programme is available at https://www.bbc.co.uk/programmes/p01sh4on (accessed 12 November 2018).
30. Ministry of Defence, *Soldiering – The Military Covenant*, Army Doctrine Publication, No. 5, 1–2, https://assets.publishing.service.gov.uk/government/uploads/system/uploads/attachment_data/file/395358/2000-ADPvol5_Soldiering_the_Military_Covenant_Ver2.pdf (accessed 12 November 2018). The Armed Forces Act 2011 applied the Covenant to all services.
31. John Milton, *Samson Agonistes*, l.1758, in *The Poems of John Milton*, ed. John Carey and Alistair Fowler (London: Longmans, Green and Co, 1968), 402.
32. Ridden, 'The Bard's Speech', n.p.
33. Tim Prentki and Sheila Preston, 'Applied Theatre: An Introduction', in Prentki and Preston, *The Applied Theatre Reader*, 16.

Afterword

Rowan Mackenzie

Applied and socially engaged Shakespeare continues to develop and evolve – a dynamic field that responds to the needs of participants as they navigate through a challenging world that often excludes them in both conscious and unconscious ways. This volume began life in the Applying Shakespeare Symposia that took place, respectively, at the Shakespeare Institute, University of Birmingham, and the University of Surrey in 2018 and 2019. The conversations during these events ranged from working with Shakespeare with children with learning disabilities to programmes to engage those from socially disadvantaged backgrounds, from professional actors with Downs syndrome to work in carceral settings. The discussions were rich, varied and filled with enthusiasm for the way in which applied Shakespeare can open up new opportunities for those involved, bringing together academics, practitioners and participants to examine the usage and the potential for future developments. Since that time the world has undergone significant change. The outbreak of the COVID-19 pandemic, Brexit, the war in Ukraine and many other sociopolitical impacts have altered the landscape of life for almost

Notes for this section begin on page 165.

all of us. The relevance of this work has perhaps never been more apparent than in the aftermath of these fundamental changes, as people attempt to navigate their way through a vastly altered world.

Many of those who work in applied theatre have seen significant professional challenges over recent years. COVID-19 caused widespread suspension of in-person events for much of 2020–21 due to lockdowns and continued uncertainty for productions even as the restrictions eased. There was significantly increased competition for funding: Arts Council England reported receipt of 13,688 applications for emergency funding in a three-week period during the early months of the pandemic, compared to a typical annualised figure of 14,000 grant applications.[1] Gavin Williamson's contentious decision to reduce funding for arts and humanities qualifications by 50 per cent in 2021 meant that many universities have removed or closed courses in these areas, causing redundancies among staff and reduced opportunities for future creative artists.[2] Brexit has decimated the sources of European Funding that many projects were reliant upon (an average of £40 million per annum since 2007) and the restrictions on travel and work have impacted negatively on artists' 'emotional, creative and financial' well-being.[3] Russia's invasion of Ukraine has been catastrophic for those caught up in the fighting and for the wider Ukrainian population, including academics and artists, a number of whom spoke eloquently about the impact during the Shakespeare Beyond Borders Alliance Equality Shakespeare Festival in May 2022.[4] The 2022 cost of living crisis driven by increased prices of energy, fuel and consumer goods has resulted in inflation exceeding 10 per cent, spiralling numbers of low-income households falling into poverty, reduced spending on non-essential items and increased reliance on foodbanks for many.[5] This background of economic challenges, the emotional toll of many of those changes and the reduced opportunity for creative work have meant that many theatre and applied theatre projects have been negatively affected.

Yet throughout the challenges of this period socially engaged Shakespeare has continued to develop and flourish around the globe. As Kathleen Gallagher affirms, 'the relational aspects of drama are one of its strengths', and these strengths are perhaps needed more than ever against the backdrop of political turmoil, economic instability, social injustice and emotional turbulence that is emblematic of the world today.[6] It is this ability for drama to be used as a way of building and strengthening relationships that makes it so powerful during times of stress, exclusion and division. Ann Dutlinger was writing about the Second World War when she described how

> individual identity could be reclaimed – albeit momentarily – through art ... The act of making art suspended the collective nightmare ... it helped to sustain hope, a sense of self, and the will to live.[7]

However, this is equally applicable to any situation where individuals feel that their identity is compromised and that they need to find a creative outlet to enable them to sustain hope during the challenges of a collective nightmare. Mark Fleishman writes that 'theatre and performance more broadly are commonly understood to be collective practices in which a community of some kind is brought into being albeit for a limited period of time'.[8] It is this sense of community that makes drama such a powerful tool to create meaningful social engagement during times of significant challenges, whether individually or collectively.

This collection focuses on a diverse range of communities that have been brought into being through the medium of Shakespeare, some for brief periods of time, such as the Most Mira projects in Bosnia, and others for years, as is the case with Blue Apple Theatre Company. Whether the community is formed for hours, days, weeks, months or years, the impact often far outlives the culmination of the work, inspiring those who have participated to see themselves and the world refracted through a different lens. Through exploring the world via the medium of characters rather than improvisational drama using their own life experiences, both participants and audiences of these applied Shakespeare programmes are encouraged to consider perspectives that may otherwise have been unknown to them. Sue Jennings has described this concept as 'dramatic distancing',[9] as it enables those involved to explore the world through fictional characters that may allow them to consider circumstances that would be too difficult, challenging or painful to consider closely if they were related directly to their own experiences. Dramatic distancing can apply with any text-based theatrical work, and is not specific to Shakespeare, yet Shakespeare does in many ways elicit a response unlike that of any other playwright.

The question of what it is that makes Shakespeare unique is a complex one that goes beyond the scope of this collection and has been the subject of academic deliberation for centuries. However, within the context of applied Shakespeare, there are some elements that can be identified as common threads among a multitude of projects. Shakespeare's work, with its inherent 'cultural capital',[10] can be seen as problematic and having contributed to the marginalisation of many groups through the exclusivity it naturally invokes. However, the inversion or 'leveraging [of] the cultural currency of Shakespeare'[11] can utilise this same exclusivity as a tool for social change through adding validity to contemporary issues. Shakespeare can encourage a wider (and often different type of) audience than would perhaps be drawn to devised pieces tackling issues of social exclusion, disabilities, incarceration and ecology. The work of Shakespeare can be appropriated to give voice to those who society may otherwise fail to hear or to acknowledge; it can be used as a methodology for conveying messages about peace in post-war communities, the impacts of climate change on the most vulnerable within society or the dehumanising effects of imprisonment on individuals' ability to create a non-offending identity.

Those involved in the creation of such theatre can establish their own community through the experience of the creative process and the sharing of ownership of these canonical works to articulate their own stories through the medium of Shakespeare. For audiences of Shakespeare adapted and performed by marginalised communities or tackling issues of marginalisation, the experience can alter their previously held perceptions of theatre and the way it can be used to speak to modern social issues. The heterotopic qualities of applied Shakespeare can encourage audiences to challenge their own perceptions of those involved, asking them to 'look beyond the labels, see behind the stigma and see something more'[12] as a result of the unexpected juxtaposition of Shakespeare and marginalised performers. As one invited guest commented following a production of *The Tempest* in an English prison:

> The benefits are endless – the chance to feel 'normal and like a human being' (one of them said this to me) is crucial to their time in custody, a chance to be creative, to be themselves and enjoy what they are doing – it is so important.[13]

It is not only the performing of Shakespeare that can have a significant impact – the use of it as a learning tool can also bridge divides within society, whether of the type explored by Cavanagh and Rowland in their inclusive Shakespeare curriculum that exchanges writing between college students and incarcerated students, or the connections between D/deaf and hearing children through their educational experiences of Shakespeare, as Rokison-Woodall and Irish explore in their chapter. While Shakespeare can and has been used as a way of causing division through the exclusive nature of cultural capital, oppression and *othering*, it can also be used as a way of creating dialogue in a universal language that can focus on our shared humanity rather than our respective differences. The examples of applied and socially engaged Shakespeare within this volume use the characters, language and legacy to celebrate our individuation and explore the often challenging and problematic issues that are central to our current situation.

Rowan Mackenzie is both practitioner and academic, working with specialised communities. Her doctoral research used spatial theory as a framework to examine global theatre practices with incarcerated people and people with mental health issues, learning disabilities and experiences of homelessness. She is founder and Artistic Director of Shakespeare UnBard, which facilitates collaborative theatre companies in a number of UK prisons, and Co-Chair of the Shakespeare Beyond Borders Alliance. She is the recipient of many national and international awards for her work, including the prestigious Butler Trust award. She has published numerous chapters and essays on Shakespeare within prisons, Shakespeare with learning-disabled actors and the heterotopic potential of applied theatre. Her monograph *Creating Space for Shakespeare* was published by Bloomsbury Arden in March 2023.

Notes

1. Arts Council England, 'Emergency Response Funds', https://www.artscouncil.org.uk/covid19/emergency-response-funds (accessed 30 September 2022).
2. Sally Weale, 'Funding Cuts to Go Ahead for University Arts Courses in England Despite Opposition', *Guardian*, 20 July 2021, https://www.theguardian.com/education/2021/jul/20/funding-cuts-to-go-ahead-for-university-arts-courses-in-england-despite-opposition (accessed 30 September 2022).
3. Charlotte Faucher, 'The Arts after Brexit: The Impact of the UK's Departure from the European Union on Its Cultural Relations with European Union Member States' (London: Economic and Social Research Council, November 2020), https://www.ukmusic.org/wp-content/uploads/2022/07/W-3-theartsafterbrexitfinal.pdf (accessed 30 September 2022).

4. Professor Michael Dobson in conversation with Professor Nataliya Torkut, Professor Maya Harbuzyuk, Professor Natalia Vysotsla and Dr Daria Moskvitina, 'Shakespeare in Ukraine' panel, Shakespeare Beyond Borders Alliance Equality Shakespeare Festival, 24 May 2022, https://www.youtube.com/watch?v=RWwfndo2GUg (accessed 21 September 2022).
5. Brigid Francis-Devine, Paul Bolton, Matthew Keep and Daniel Harari, 'Rising Cost of Living in the UK' (London: House of Commons Library Research Briefing, 28 September 2022), https://researchbriefings.files.parliament.uk/documents/CBP-9428/CBP-9428.pdf (accessed 8 October 2022).
6. Kathleen Gallagher, 'The Micro-Political and the Socio-Structural in Applied Theatre with Homeless Youth', in Jenny Hughes and Helen Nicholson (eds), *Critical Perspectives on Applied Theatre* (Cambridge: Cambridge University Press, 2016), 229–47, here 230.
7. Anne Dutlinger, *Art, Music and Education as a Strategy for Survival: 194:–1945* (New York: Herodias, 2011), 5.
8. Mark Fleishman, 'Applied Theatre and Participation in the "New" South Africa: A Possible Politics', in Jenny Hughes and Helen Nicholson (eds), *Critical Perspectives on Applied Theatre* (Cambridge: Cambridge University Press, 2016), 193–211, here 195.
9. Sue Jennings, *Dramatherapy: Theory and Practice 2* (London: Routledge, 1992), 17.
10. Pierre Bourdieu, 'The Forms of Capital' (trans. Richard Nice), in J. Richardson (ed.), *Handbook of Theory and Research for the Sociology of Education* (Westport, CT: Greenwood, 1986), 241–58, here 241.
11. Paul Prescott, 'Shakespearean Environmentalism and Ecology: Shakespeare in Yosemite' panel, Shakespeare Beyond Borders Alliance Equality Shakespeare Festival, 15 June 2022, https://www.youtube.com/watch?v=2cUn6clcGrc&list=PL5TjiPIpilP8sxmZRs9w7Ft2Z-GW_h1lr&index=18 (accessed 2 November 2022).
12. Keith, an actor in The Gallowfield Players (a collaborative theatre company in an English prison formed of 15 inmates and Rowan Mackenzie), speech given after the performance of *Julius Caesar* (June 2019).
13. Audience feedback following Emergency Shakespeare's production of *The Tempest* (prison theatre company in an English prison) (July 2022).

Index

Adams, Robert, 132, 145
Adieshiah, Sian, 55, 67
Adoption and Safe Families Act, 120
Aebischer, Pascale, 158
Ahmed, Syed Jamil, 32
American Shakespeare Company, 160
Arbus, Arin, 74–5
Arrowsmith, Charlotte, 142
Arts Council England, 162, 165
Ash, Melanie, 67

B., 125
Bachman, Ronet, 129
Bade, William F., 33
Bagnall, Nick, 55
Balfour, Michael, 106
Barnard, Philip, 6
Barry, Becky, 142
Bar-Tal, Daniel, 48
Barton, John, 67
Bates, Laura, 70, 83, 95, 105
Beale, Simon Russell, 144
Beaudouin, Tariq, 80
Beck, Rupert, 67
Belloni, Roberto, 48
Bennett, Peter, 129
Bennink, Gemma, 48
Berry, Cicely, 67, 95, 105, 136, 146
Bevis, Matthew, 44, 50

Bey, Amiti, 80, 82
Biggs, Ronnie, 69
Billy Rose Foundation, 142
Blair, Tony, 54
Blakinger, Keri, 119, 129
Blitz, Cynthia, 129
Bloom, Benjamin S., 71, 83
Blue Apple Theatre Company, 5, 153–55, 158, 160, 163
Boal, Augusto, 92, 113, 116, 125, 129
Bodinetz, Gemma, 66
Bolton, Paul, 166
Borallon Training and Correctional Centre, 90, 103
Bottoms, Stephen, 32
Bourdieu, Pierre, 166
Bragg, Bernard, 146
Braidwood Trust School for the Deaf, 132, 145
Braidwood, Thomas, 132
Bralo, Zrikna, 49
Brayton, Dan, 32
Bristol, Michael D., 62, 68
British Association of Teachers of Deaf Children and Young People, 145
British Deaf Association, 145
Broadmoor Hospital, 149
Brokaw, Katherine Steele, 3, 17–33
Bronte, Emily
    Wuthering Heights, 62

Index

Brook, Peter, 150
Brooks, Ernest C., 72
Brown, Eric C., 159
Browning, Peter, 33
Bruckner, Lyn, 32
Burbles, Nicholas, 67
Burnett, Mark Thornton, 159
Burns, Ken, 26
Busuttil, Walter, 156
Byron, Sammie, 72, 103

Calarco, Jessica McCrory, 60, 67
California Lawyers for the Arts, 72
Camus, J. 145
Carey, John, 160
Casper, 79
Cavanagh, Sheila T., 4, 69–74, 164
Cayton, H., 145
Ceaușescu, Nicolae, 16
Cervantes, Miguel de, 75
Chedgzoy, Kate, 158
Chekhov, Michael, 115, 116
Chernomyrdin, Viktor, 35
Chilton, Helen, 137–38, 140, 146
Chirac, Jacques, 35
Clean Break, 101
Clerke, Peter, 154
Clinton, Bill, 35
Cobb, Hal, 152
Cobb, Jelani, 113
Cochrane, Claire, 62, 68
Coltrane, John, 75
Combat Stress, 156
Combat Veteran Players, 155–57, 160
Conquergood, Dwight, 3, 19, 21
Cox, Murray, 149, 159
Coyle, Andrew, 119, 129
Crewe, Ben, 122, 129
Cumberbatch, Benedict, 51
Davis, Gordon, 32
Dayton Peace Accord, 35, 48
Deafinitely, 133
Demastes, William W., 45, 50
Detroit Public Theatre, 108, 128
Dewey, John, 59, 67

Diaz, Sabrina, 25
Dietz, Steven
   Becky's New Car, 128
Diklić, Davor, 50
Dionne, Craig, 32
Dobson, Michael, 65–66, 68, 144, 149, 166
Donmar Warehouse, 54, 66
   All-female Trilogy, 66
Donnelly, Madaline, 160
Down, John Langdon, 155
Dreyfus, Hubert L., 103
Duggan, Patrick, 50
Duncan, Sandy, 128
Dutlinger, Ann, 163, 166
Dworin, Judy, 113

Elden, Stuart, 101
Ellis, Neville, 66
Emergency Shakespeare, 94, 105, 166
Etherton, Michael, 63, 66, 68
Eustis, Oskar, 66

Faber, Amanda, 160
Falconer, Karl, 4, 51–68
Farrell, James, 65
Faucher, Charlotte, 165
Fendler, Lyn, 67
Ferguson, Donna, 67
Fischer, Anastasia A., 129
Fischer, Martina, 48
Fleishman, Mark, 163, 166
Flynn, Molly, 68
Foucault, Michel, 4, 85–87, 90 101–3
Fowler, Alistair, 160
Francis, Becky, 66
Francis-Devine, Brigid, 166

Gallagher, Kathleen, 162, 166
Gallowfield Players, 166
Gardner, Lyn, 66
Geese Theatre, 92, 104
Gelt, Jessica, 66
Globe to Globe Festival, 75, 80

Greenhalgh, Susanne, 5, 147–60
Greunewald, David, 52, 66
Grint, William, 142

Haeckel, Ernst, 20
Hall, Ian, 67
Harari, Daniel, 166
Harbuzyuk, Maya, 166
Harpin, Anna, 32
Hatton, Diane C., 129
Heddon, Deirdre, 32
Herold, Neils, 6, 152, 160
Hinsliff, Gaby, 67
HMP Gartree, 102
HMP Leicester, 5, 88–100, 103, 106
HMP Wandsworth, 69–70
Hodzic, Refik, 35
Höfele, Andreas, 103
Holdsworth, Nadine, 68
Honigmann, E.A.J., 102
Honneth, Axel, 68
Horrox, Katarina, 103
Hotakainen, Rob, 32
Houseman, Barbara, 67
Huang, Alexa, 159
Hughes, Jenny, 32, 166
Humanity in Action, 39
Hunter, Kelly, 8, 16, 65
Huron Valley Correctional Facility, 107–8

Inside Out, 156–7
International Centre for Criminal Justice, 35
Irish, Tracy, 5, 65, 130–46, 165
Izetbegović, Alija, 35

J., 125
Jackson, Shannon, 30, 33
Jacobs, Michael, 93, 105
James, 154
Jarvis, Peter, 61, 68
Jennings, Sue Emmy, 3, 7–16, 103, 163, 166
Jensen, Michael P., 149–50, 159
Jessop, Jane, 153

Jessop, Tommy, 153–5
Jessop, William
　Growing Up Down's, 5, 153–55, 158
　Living Without Fear, 155
Johnson, E. Patrick, 31
Johnson, Peter, 101
Johnson, Shelton, 26–7
Johnston, Paul, 102
Jones, Charlotte
　Humble Boy, 128

Katie, 154–55
Keehan, Bridget, 105
Keep, Matthew, 166
Keith, 166
Kershaw, Baz, 32
Klaić, Dragan, 40
Kohl, Helmut, 35
Kolb, David, 55
Kolluru, Akhila, 82
Kostić, Laza, 49
Kozusko, Matt, 148, 150, 159
Krathwohl, David R., 83
Kray, Reggie, 69
Kray, Ronnie, 69
Kuftinec, Sonja Arsham, 49
Kwei-Armah, Kwame, 66

L., 115
Lansburgh Theatre, 160
Lavender, Andy, 17, 31
Lawrie, 154, 155
Lederach, John Paul, 48
Ledgard, Chris
　And Calm of Mind, 156–7
Lefebvre, Henri, 4, 86–89, 91–92, 95–96, 101–3
Lehmann, Courtney, 148, 159
Leland, Dorothy, 25
Letts, Tracy
　Superior Donuts, 117
Library of Congress, 80
Linklater, Kristin, 115, 122, 129
Liverpool Everyman, 54–55, 66
Liverpool Playhouse, 66

Lloyd, Phyllida, 66
Lough, Catherine, 68
Loughland, Tony, 66
Loveday, Vik, 60, 67
Lucas, Ashley, 109
Luhrmann, Baz, 159
Luther Luckett Correctional Complex, 72, 151–3
Lynch, Loretta, 120, 129

Mackenzie, Rowan, 4, 6, 65, 85–106, 161–6
Mackey, Sally, 32
Magenta Giraffe Theatre Company, 108
Magill, Tom, 95, 105
Major, John, 35
Marshall, Penny, 48
Martin, Randall, 20–21, 24, 31–32
Maruschak, Laura M., 129
Marx, Karl, 33
Masia, Bertram B., 83
Matt, 116, 117
May, Theresa J., 20, 32
Mayer, Connie, 146
McCracken, Wendy, 146
McKellen, Ian, 159
McLaughlin, Stewart, 69, 83
McLean, Kwame, 80
McLoughlin, Jaclyn, 155–56, 160
Meladrama, 55–57, 59, 64–5
Milatović-Ovadia, Maja, 3, 34–50
Mills, Enos, 25
Mills, Hayley, 128
Milošević, Slobodan, 35
Milton, John
 Samson Agonistes, 156, 160
Minnesota Correctional Facility, 108
Miskowiec, Jay, 101
Monroe Correctional Facility, 4, 70–82
Moore, Gerald, 101
Moore, John, 101
Morreall, John, 50
Moskvitina, Daria, 166

Most Mira, 3, 34–50, 163
 Shakespeare's Comedies, 34–47
 Shakespeare's Fools, 3, 39–44, 47
Muir, John, 3, 17–18, 21, 23–30
Mullaney, Steven, 103
Murphy, Andrew, 54, 66–67

National Deaf Children's Society, 132
National Theatre, 53, 128
Nice, Richard, 166
Nicholson, Helen, 1, 6, 19–20, 31–32, 40, 68, 148, 159, 166
Nicholson-Smith, Donald, 101, 102, 103
Normansfield Theatre, 155
Northern Broadsides, 65
Novis, Phil, 96, 102, 106

O'Dair, Sharon, 30, 33, 67, 91, 103
O'Hanlan, Jacqui, 133, 145
O'Malley, Evelyn, 20, 24, 31–32
Osborne, Laurie, 158
Overton, Shawn, 25, 27

Papp, Joe, 21
Paton, Graeme, 66
Paul Hamlyn Foundation, 65
Peacock, Louise, 50
Pensalfini, Rob, 6, 103, 105, 109–10, 128, 150, 153, 159–60
Perry, Emma, 66
Peschel, Lisa, 50
Petit, Lenard, 129
Petrovic-Ziemer, Ljubinka, 48
Petty, Geoff, 67
Popkewitz, Thomas, 67
Porges, Stephen, 121, 129
Powers, Kate, 5, 107–29
Prendergast, Monica, 63, 68,
Prentki, Tim, 42, 44, 50, 66, 68, 158–60
Prescott, John, 54, 67
Prescott, Paul, 3, 17–33, 166
Preston, Sheila, 158–60
Prisoner Learning Alliance, 101

Public Theatre, 21, 66
Purewal, Sandeep, 54, 63, 66, 68
PurpleCoat, 4, 52–68

Queensland Shakespeare Ensemble, 90, 103

Rabinow, Paul, 102–3
Rai, Milan, 67
Rancière, Jacques, 55
Ray, James Earl, 69
Redeeming Time Project, 108, 111–18, 128
Rehabilitation Through the Arts (RTA), 74, 108, 112, 114, 122
Richards, Jamie, 25
Richardson, John G., 166
Ridden, Geoffrey, 150–51, 158–60
Riley, Kristi, 129
Rivas, Jessica, 23
Rivier, Estelle, 159
Rivlin, Elizabeth, 159
Robinson, Lee, 137, 146
Rodenburg, Patsy, 67, 115, 129
Rogerson, Hank
  Shakespeare Behind Bars, 5, 84, 103, 151–54, 157
Rokison-Woodall, Abigail, 5, 65, 130–46, 165
Rose Theatre, Kingston, 155, 158
Rowland, Steve, 4, 69–84, 164
  Time Out of Joint, 75, 79, 83
Royal Shakespeare Company, 2, 5, 53, 60–61, 65, 130–35, 141–44
Rubio-Garrido, Alberto, 103
Rufford, Juliet, 61, 67
Ryan, Natasha, 59–63, 67

S., 124–5
Sandole, Denise J. D., 48
Saxton, Juliana, 63, 68,
Schechner, Richard, 49, 148–49, 158–59
Schininà, Guglielmo, 149, 159
Scott-Douglas, Amy, 6
Seeley, A., 145

Shackleton, Steve, 25
Shailor, Jonathan, 104, 109, 128–29
Shakespeare Behind Bars, 72, 101, 103
Shakespeare Beyond Borders Alliance, 162, 165–66
Shakespeare in Prison (SIP), 108–18, 123–26, 128
  Richard III in Prison: A Critical Edition, 109
Shakespeare Lives, 160
Shakespeare North Playhouse, 65
Shakespeare Reclaimed, 109
Shakespeare Schools Festival, 52
Shakespeare UnBard, 165
Shakespeare, William
  As You Like It, 18, 26–27, 44
  The Comedy of Errors, 160
  Coriolanus, 74
  Hamlet, 5, 39, 74, 79, 82, 150, 153–55, 157, 159
  Henry IV, Part 1, 78, 92
  Henry IV, Part 2, 92
  Henry V, 115, 152, 155–7
  Julius Caesar, 74, 166
  King Lear, 22, 41–44, 47, 74, 153
  Macbeth, 55, 57, 62, 74, 77, 79, 102, 130–31, 137–43
  Measure for Measure, 74, 80–81
  The Merchant of Venice, 74, 77, 79
  A Midsummer Night's Dream, 3, 7–16, 18, 32, 34, 39, 40–41, 46, 72, 153, 155
  Much Ado about Nothing, 153
  Othello, 5, 54, 66, 74, 88–100, 102, 104–5, 159
  Richard II, 28
  Richard III, 109, 155
  Romeo and Juliet, 28, 33, 39, 77, 79
  The Tempest, 41–43, 74, 151–53, 164, 166
  Timon of Athens, 28, 33
  Titus Andronicus, 159
  Troilus and Cressida, 25

Twelfth Night, 32, 54, 66, 79, 118, 124–26, 155
The Winter's Tale, 93
Shakespeare's Globe, 2, 75, 80, 144, 155, 157–58
Shakur, Tupac, 81
Shapiro, Lawrence, 136, 146
Shaughnessy, Nicola, 6
Shaughnessy, Robert, 1–6, 65, 106, 158–59
Shaw, George Bernard, 22
Shepherd-Bates, Frannie, 5, 107–29
Sheridan, Alan, 102
Shi, Jing, 129
Siegel, Jane, 129
Signing Shakespeare, 130–46
Sing Sing Correctional Facility, 108, 117, 128
Singh, Mohendra, 80, 82
Smallman, Emma, 104
Smith, Alan, 129
Smith, Holly-Rae, 67
Snow, Georgia, 66
Snyder, Susan, 142
Soja, Edward W., 87–88, 102
Soldier's Arts Academy, 160
South Sierra Miwuk, 23
South Sierra Paiute, 23
Steingraber, Sandra, 28
Stetson, Lee, 24–26, 28
Stewart, J.I.M., 93, 104
Stewart, Patrick, 51
Stojanovic, Dubravka, 48
STOLL, 155
Stolz, Steven A., 136, 146
Stredder, James, 146
Strupinskienė, Lina, 48
Stuart, Mel
  The Hobart Shakespeareans, 159
Subramanian, Ram, 129
Swavola, Elizabeth, 119, 129
Sykes, Gresham M., 129

Takkal, Aixa, 103
Tandy, Miles, 55, 67
Taylor, Gary, 159
Theater for a New Audience, 74
Theatre Aspen, 128
Thomas, Eva, 82
Thompson, James, 2, 3, 6, 19–20, 31, 40, 44, 49–50, 149, 158–59
Thorpe, Vanessa, 66
Tilsey, Thomas, 131
Tim, 117
Time Out of Joint, 71, 79–2
TIPP, 101
Tofteland, Curt R. 72–73, 84, 109, 123, 151–2
Torku, Nataliya, 166
Trounstine, Jean, 6
Tudjman, Franjo, 35

Üngör, Ugur Umit, 45, 50
United Service Organisation, 160

van der Merwe, Hugo, 48
Van Meter, Matthew, 126
Verkerke, Valerie Amandine, 45, 50
Vockins, Katherine, 74, 108
Vulliamy, Ed, 48
Vygotsky, Lev, 146
Vysotsla, Natalia, 166

Waldman, Michael
  My Shakespeare, 159
Wallace, Matt, 152, 160
Wanamaker, Sam, 31
Warr, Jason, 129
Weale, Sally, 165
Wells, Stanley, 159
West Shoreline Correctional Facilities, 72
Westby, Carol, 137, 146
Whittlesey, Josie, 75
Wilde, Oscar, 69
William James Association, 72
Williams, Ian, 48
Williamson, Gavin, 162
Wilson, August, 75
Winston, Joe, 55, 67

Wolff, Nancy, 120, 129
Woodbourne Correctional Facility, 71, 74, 80
Woolf, Virginia
  To the Lighthouse, 62, 68
Wootten, Angie, 133–35, 145
World Earth Day, 3, 24
World Shakespeare Project, 71, 83
Wray, Ramona, 159

York, Michael, 159
Yosemite National Park, 3, 17–33
  One Touch of Nature, 24–30
Young Vic, 66
Young, Caroline, 81, 84

Zeilizer, Craig, 49
Živojinić, Velimir, 49

www.ingramcontent.com/pod-product-compliance
Lightning Source LLC
Chambersburg PA
CBHW072053110526
44590CB00018B/3158